UNLEASHED

Releasing God's Glorious Kingdom in and Through You

BIBLE STUDY GUIDE | SIX SESSIONS

Tony Evans

HarperChristian Resources

CONTENTS

A NOTE FROM TONY EVANS

Dear friend,

If there's one thing I want you to know before we begin this journey together, it's this: *You were never meant to live a powerless Christian life.* You were created to walk in victory, purpose, and spiritual authority—not someday, but right now.

That's because the kingdom of God is not just "up there," waiting for you in the sweet by-and-by. Jesus Himself said "the kingdom of God is at hand" (Mark 1:15). That means His rule, His presence, and His power are available to you today. But here's the key: His kingdom power is only experienced when His kingdom is prioritized.

That's what this study is all about. We're not just chasing inspiration; we're going after transformation. Real change happens when you align yourself under God's rule and live out His kingdom agenda in every area of life. As you do, you unleash His power in ways you never imagined.

We'll look at what it means to live under divine authority. We'll explore how to tap into the resources of heaven through the work of the Holy Spirit. And we'll dig deep into how God's truth anchors you when the culture around you keeps shifting. This isn't about religion. It's about a relationship that results in representation—your life as a living testimony to the rule of the King.

But I want to warn you up front—this study is going to challenge you. Because if you want to live unleashed, you've got to be willing to let go of anything that's been holding you back. That may mean reordering your priorities, renewing your mind, or recommitting your heart. But know this: The freedom, peace, and power that come from living in alignment with the kingdom are more than worth it.

So as you begin, I pray you'll lean in with an open heart and a teachable spirit. I believe that as you commit to seeking first the kingdom of God, everything else you've been chasing will start to fall into place—just as Jesus promised (see Matthew 6:33).

Let's get started. Heaven is closer than you think.

For His kingdom,

DR. TONY EVANS

HOW TO USE THIS GUIDE

Too many believers today are living beneath their spiritual privileges. They have access to the kingdom of God through Jesus, yet they're experiencing defeat, frustration, and powerlessness in their daily lives. Like passengers stuck in coach when they have first-class tickets, they're settling for a cramped, uncomfortable spiritual journey when God has provided an upgrade to kingdom authority, peace, and power.

The problem isn't that God is withholding His blessings; it's that many Christians don't understand how to access what He's already made available. They're trying to live by the world's rules while claiming citizenship in God's kingdom. This is the purpose of this study—to help you discover how to unleash God's transforming power in every area of your life by learning to live under His kingdom authority and agenda.

Before you begin, know that there are a few ways you can go through this material. You can experience this study with others in a group (such as a Bible study, Sunday school class, or other gathering), or you can go through the content on your own. Either way, the videos are available to view at any time by following the instructions provided with this study guide.

GROUP STUDY

Each session is divided into two parts: (1) a group study section and (2) a personal study section. The group study section provides a basic framework on how to open your time together, get the most out of the video content, and discuss the key ideas that were presented in the teaching. Each session includes the following:

- **Welcome:** A short opening note about the topic of the session for you to read on your own before you meet as a group.

- **Connect:** A few icebreaker questions to get you and your group members thinking about the topic and interacting with each other.
- **Watch:** An outline of the key points covered in each video teaching along with space for you to take notes as you watch each session.
- **Discuss:** Questions to help you and your group reflect on the teaching material presented and apply it to your lives.
- **Respond:** A short personal exercise to help reinforce the key ideas.
- **Pray:** Some ideas for how to close out your group time in prayer.

If you are doing this study in a group, have your own copy of the study guide so you can write down your thoughts, responses, and reflections—and so you have access to the videos via streaming. You will also want to have a copy of the book *Unleashed*, as reading it alongside this guide will provide you with deeper insights. (See the notes at the beginning of each group session and personal study section on which chapters of the book you should read before the next group session.)

Finally, keep these points in mind:

- **Facilitation:** If you are doing this study in a group, you will want to appoint someone to serve as a facilitator. This person will be responsible for starting the video and keeping track of time during discussions and activities. If you have been chosen for this role, there are some resources in the back of this guide that can help you lead your group through the study.

- **Commitment:** Your group is a place where tremendous growth can happen as you reflect on the Bible, ask questions, and learn what God is doing in other people's lives. For this reason, be fully committed and attend each session so you can build trust and rapport with the other members.

- **Community:** The goal of any small group is to serve as a place where people can share, learn about God, and build friendships. So make your group a safe place. Be honest about your thoughts and feelings but also listen to everyone else's thoughts, feelings, and opinions. Keep anything personal that your group members share in confidence so that you can create a community where people can heal, be challenged, and grow spiritually.

If you are going through this study on your own, read the opening Welcome section and reflect on the questions in the Connect section. Watch the video and use the prompts provided to take notes. Finally, personalize the questions and exercises in the Discuss and Respond sections. Close by writing down any requests that you want to pray about during the upcoming week.

PERSONAL STUDY

The personal study is for you to work through on your own during the week. Each exercise is designed to help you explore the key ideas you uncovered during your group time and delve into passages of Scripture that will help you apply those principles to your life. Go at your own pace, doing a little each day—or tackle the material all at once. Remember to spend a few moments in silence to listen to whatever God might be saying to you.

Note that if you are doing this study as part of a group, and you are unable to finish (or even start) these personal studies for the week, you should still attend the group time. Be assured that you are still wanted and welcome even if you don't have your "homework" done. The group studies and personal studies are intended to help you hear what God wants you to hear and learn how to apply what He is saying to your life. As you go through this study, be listening for Him to speak to you about un-leashing His kingdom power and authority in every area of your life.

BEFORE GROUP MEETING	Read chapters 1–2 in *Unleashed* Read the Welcome section (page 2)
GROUP MEETING	Discuss the Connect questions Watch the video teaching for session 1 Discuss the questions that follow as a group Do the closing exercise and pray (pages 2–6)
STUDY 1	Complete the personal study (pages 9–11)
STUDY 2	Complete the personal study (pages 12–14)
STUDY 3	Complete the personal study (pages 15–18)
CATCH UP AND READ AHEAD (BEFORE WEEK 2 GROUP MEETING)	Connect with someone in your group Read chapter 3 in *Unleashed* Complete any unfinished personal studies (page 19)

EMPOWERED BY HEAVEN

[Power + Authority]

"But you will receive power when the Holy Spirit has come upon you; and you shall be My witnesses . . . as far as the remotest part of the earth."

ACTS 1:8

WELCOME | READ ON YOUR OWN

There's a difference between knowing about power and actually walking in it. Far too many Christians today live beneath their spiritual privileges—not because God's power isn't available but because they haven't learned how to access it.

They're showing up in church, reading their Bibles, maybe even praying, but they're still spiritually tired, emotionally worn out, and unsure how to move forward. That's because power is only released when we come under divine authority.

Jesus didn't tell His disciples to go out and change the world in their own strength. He told them to wait—to pause—until they received power from the Holy Spirit. Why? Because God's kingdom is not built by human effort. It is built through kingdom alignment. When you align your life under God's rule, you position yourself to receive all that heaven has already made available. That's when power shows up—power for your marriage, your calling, your decisions, and your daily battles.

The goal of this session is to help you recognize what's already within reach. The kingdom of God is not far off—it's at hand. It's available. It's alive. And the Spirit of God is ready to move in you and through you, not just for your benefit but also for the advancement of His glory on earth. If you're ready to live unleashed, it starts right here—with a decision to come under God's rule so that His power can be released through you.

CONNECT | 10 MINUTES

If you or any of your group members don't know each other, take a few minutes to introduce yourselves. Then discuss one or both of the following questions:

- Why did you decide to join this study? What do you hope to learn?

  — *or* —

- In your spiritual life right now, would you say you are running on full power, low battery, or feeling unplugged? Explain your response.

WATCH | 25 MINUTES

Watch the video for this session, which you can access by playing the DVD or through streaming (see the instructions provided with this guide). Below is an outline of the key points covered during the teaching. Record any key concepts that stand out to you.

OUTLINE

I. The kingdom of God is God's house.
   A. Just like a football team defends their "house," so God claims authority over His creation.
   B. The kingdom of God is the realm where God's rule is recognized and obeyed—both in heaven and on earth, now and forever.
   C. Acts 1:3 tells us that after His resurrection, Jesus spent forty days teaching His disciples about the kingdom of God. That was His priority.

II. Power and authority belong to the kingdom.
   A. To live unleashed, we must understand the authority and power we've been given as part of God's kingdom.
   B. Many of us don't experience God's power because we're not living under His rule.
   C. Acts begins and ends with the message of the kingdom—it's central to how God wants His people to live.

III. The Holy Spirit brings kingdom power.
   A. In Acts 1:8, Jesus promised power through the Holy Spirit for every believer.
   B. Conversion brings you into the kingdom; the Holy Spirit activates kingdom power within you.
   C. Like a D-line switch in football, the Spirit moves you from salvation into spiritual impact.

IV. Power must be activated through authority.
   A. The power is available to you, but you must flip the switch by aligning with God's authority.
   B. Just like electricity won't power your appliances unless you plug them in, kingdom power won't flow if you don't step into your authorization.

V. How do you use kingdom authority?
   A. Jesus' words in Mark 11 give us three ways to exercise kingdom power:
      1. **Pronouncement:** Speak to the mountain. Declare God's truth over your challenge.

3

2. **Prayer:** Bring God into it. Talk to Him about the mountain you've spoken to.
3. **Pardon:** Forgive. Unforgiveness blocks kingdom authority from operating in your life.

VI. You've been authorized. Now unleash it.

   A. You don't need more power; you need to activate what you've already been given.

   B. When you speak in faith, pray in alignment, and walk in forgiveness, the kingdom flows through you.

   C. You may feel small, but like a hydrant connected to a dam, you can gush God's power when you're open and aligned.

NOTES

_____

_____

_____

_____

_____

_____

_____

_____

_____

_____

_____

_____

_____

_____

_____

_____

_____

_____

_____

_____

_____

_____

_____

_____

DISCUSS | 35 MINUTES

Discuss what you just watched by answering the following questions.

1. In this session, you explored the difference between having God's power and walking in His authority. What does that difference look like practically in a believer's daily life?

2. Read Acts 1:6–8. What do these verses teach about the Holy Spirit's role in empowering kingdom living? How does this power become visible in the life of a witness?

3. Faith in God includes speaking to the mountain, praying to God, and walking in forgiveness. Which of these steps is most challenging for you right now—and why?

4. Read Mark 11:20–24. How does this passage illustrate spiritual authority in action? What does it reveal about how faith operates beneath the surface before results are seen?

5. One takeaway from the teaching was the need for followers of Jesus to speak God's truth directly to their problems. How could changing the way you speak about your challenges impact and shift what you experience spiritually?

RESPOND | 10 MINUTES

Power without alignment achieves little because it requires connection to produce results. Living unleashed begins with submitting to God's rule and walking in the authority of Christ. This involves believing, speaking, and praying God's truth while addressing spiritual blockages like unforgiveness. Jesus provided a clear path for living in God's kingdom: speak to the mountain, trust in His power, pray with faith, and forgive freely. Following this pattern moves you from simply knowing about the kingdom to truly living it. Consider these truths as you prayerfully read the following verses and then reflect on the questions that follow.

> "Whoever says to this mountain, 'Be taken up and thrown into the sea,' and does not doubt in his heart, but believes that what he says is going to happen, it will be granted to him. Therefore, I say to you, all things for which you pray and ask, believe that you have received them, and they will be granted to you. And whenever you stand praying, forgive, if you have anything against anyone, so that your Father who is in heaven will also forgive you your offenses. But if you do not forgive, neither will your Father who is in heaven forgive your offenses."

MARK 11:23–25

What is a mountain you're facing that feels too big to move? How might speaking God's truth to that mountain, rather than just worrying about it, shift your mindset?

Is there any unforgiveness you've been holding that could be hindering your prayers? If so, what would it mean for you to release that offense and walk in freedom?

PRAY | 10 MINUTES

As you close, acknowledge God's authority over your life and thank Him for including you in His kingdom. Ask for the Holy Spirit's guidance to reconnect with His power, align with His truth, and act on the authority He has given you through faith, prayer, and forgiveness. Commit to living a life that is empowered by heaven!

PERSONAL STUDY

This week's group time introduced you to the fact that God's power is not something you earn but something you've been given. Yet it must be activated! The Holy Spirit empowers you not just to endure life but also to influence it. These daily reflections are designed to help you press further into that truth—to uncover what it means to live under God's rule, speak with bold faith, pray with confidence, and walk in forgiveness.

Take time to be honest, listen for God's voice, and expect to be challenged and changed. Also, as you work through these exercises, be sure to write down your responses to the questions, as you will be given a few minutes to share your insights in the next session if you are engaging in this study with a group. If you are reading *Unleashed* alongside this study, first review the introduction and chapters 1–2 of the book.

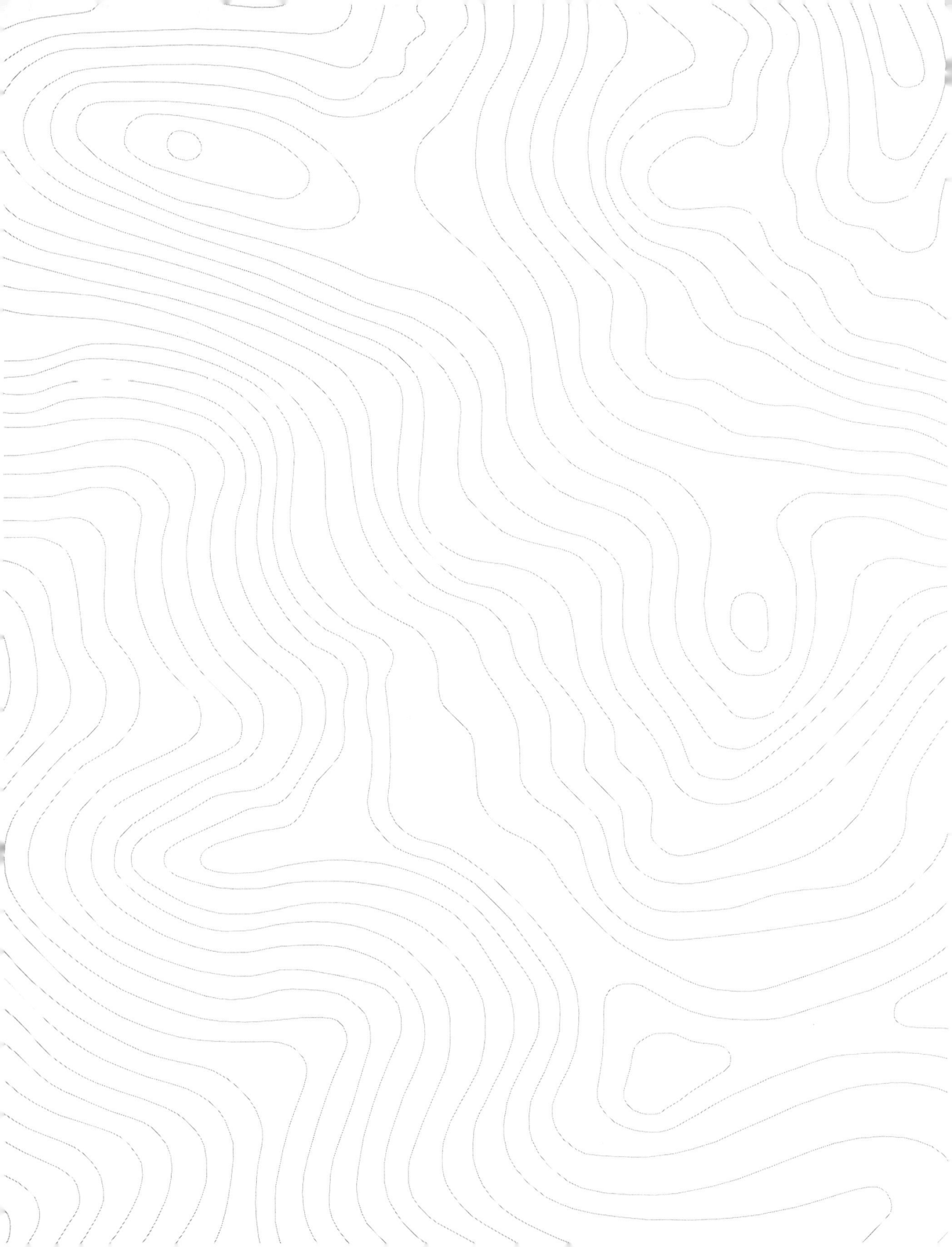

Study 1

UNDER AUTHORITY

What happens when you live in someone else's house but try to make your own rules? *Tension. Confusion. Conflict.* That's exactly what happens when believers in Christ try to live in God's kingdom without submitting to His rule.

We often ask God for strength, clarity, or breakthrough—and those are good prayers. But sometimes what we really need isn't more help from God; it's more surrender to Him. Power flows where authority is honored. That's why the first step to living unleashed isn't *doing* more but *aligning* more.

Jesus spent forty days after His resurrection speaking to His disciples about the kingdom of God. That wasn't filler content. It was preparation. He was showing them the same authority that governs heaven is now meant to govern their lives on earth. And the same is true for us.

You may be a believer in Jesus—but are you living under His rule? That's the question at the heart of this study. God's power isn't hidden from you. It's available to you. But the switch that releases it is trust. Not just general belief in God but active trust in His authority over every area of your life.

It's easy to want God's blessing while also wanting to keep the control. But control is a cheap substitute for peace—and it's a barrier to power. The Holy Spirit is more than a comforting presence. He is the dynamic force of God's rule working in you and through you. When you yield to Him, you don't lose freedom—you gain access. "Your kingdom come. Your will be done, on earth as it is in heaven" (Matthew 6:10).

Take time this week to evaluate your alignment. Not your activity. Not your performance. Just your posture. Is there any part of your life that's operating outside of God's direction? If so, that's not a place of punishment—it's an invitation.

The King is near, and He's ready to move in power. But He doesn't force His way in. He waits for surrender.

1. At what level do you feel you're under God's kingdom authority in every area of your life?

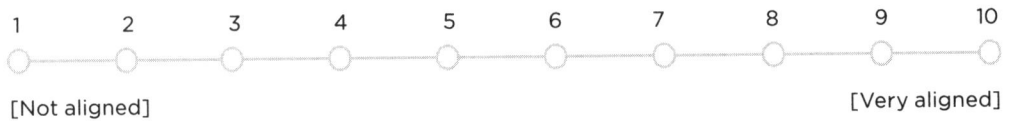

| 1 | 2 | 3 | 4 | 5 | 6 | 7 | 8 | 9 | 10 |

[Not aligned]   [Very aligned]

2. What are the biggest factors currently influencing your alignment?

Now that we understand the kingdom and God's rule, what does it mean for the kingdom of God to be at hand? For something to be at hand, it needs to be close enough to touch. Your hand is never more than a few feet from your body. Even if you were to stretch your hand as far as you possibly could, it would still be near enough to see and use. For the kingdom of God to be at hand means that God's kingdom—His rule, power, and authority— are within close proximity to each of us. When Jesus Christ came to Earth and sojourned on our planet, He brought the kingdom near to us all. Upon His resurrection, He left the Holy Spirit so that the kingdom of God and all it contains would always be accessible and close by.[1]

3. Read Luke 17:20–21. If the kingdom of God is already near and active within you through the work of the Holy Spirit, how might that change the way you approach your daily decisions, conversations, or struggles this week? Where do you need to realign with the reality that God's power is present—not distant?

4. Read Romans 12:1-2 and James 4:7-8, and then respond to the following:

> Based on these passages, what does a surrendered life look like?

> How does renewing your mind connect to experiencing God's will and walking in His power?

> What specific actions do Paul and James advise you to take? How can you apply these teachings to your life and start to take these actions this week?

No matter what section of the plane you sit in, one thing remains the same: You arrive at the same destination as everyone else on the plane. Both coach and first class always end up at the same place. The benefits of sitting in first class affect your journey, not your destination. The benefits make your journey far more pleasant, abundant, and restful. But the destination is the same as everyone else. Similarly, for those who have trusted in Jesus Christ for the salvation of their sins, the destination is the same. We will all arrive in heaven one day due to the shed blood and sacrifice of Jesus. But the journey there—your earth story—can be a far different experience depending on whether you choose to upgrade your spiritual life or travel basic economy in coach.[2]

5. Read John 18:33-37. Jesus told Pilate the kingdom of God wasn't of this world—it wasn't something physical but a spiritual realty that was already here, active, and present. How does this shift your view of God's power in your life? Where do you need to stop waiting and start living like the King is already present?

Study 2

SPEAK TO THE MOUNTAIN

Some problems don't move because we've never spoken to them in faith. In Mark 11, Jesus didn't tell the disciples to simply talk to God about the mountain—He told them to speak directly to it. This wasn't about "name it and claim it" hype. It was a *kingdom* principle. Jesus was showing them—and us—that when we are aligned with God's will, our words have spiritual weight.

Mountains in Scripture often represent obstacles that are humanly immovable. These challenges may feel too heavy to lift, too complex to solve. But Jesus said if we believe and do not doubt, we can speak to the mountain—and it will move. This isn't about pretending the problem isn't real but about declaring that God's truth is greater than the problem. We speak to our mountain with the authority God has already given us.

This principle can feel unfamiliar to us. We're used to praying quietly or waiting passively for God to act. But Jesus invites us into a more active partnership—one where we speak with kingdom confidence, not because we're powerful but because we're authorized. Speaking to the mountain doesn't mean we command God; it means we come into agreement with what He's already said.

This kind of faith doesn't come from emotion or hype but from knowing who God is, believing what He says, and staying connected to Him through prayer and surrender. The more we abide in Christ, the more clearly we hear what to speak and when to speak it. "Whoever says to this mountain, 'Be taken up and thrown into the sea,' and does not doubt in his heart, but believes that what he says is going to happen, it will be granted to him" (Mark 11:23).

This week, take note of the mountains in your life. Are there places where you've been silent when God has given you permission to speak? Start by declaring His truth—not just in your mind but out loud. Don't just describe the mountain. Direct it.

What "mountain" seems too big to move? How does aligning your words with God's Word change the way you approach prayer, spiritual warfare, or discouragement?

I. Jesus said that speaking to the "mountain"—those challenges in life that seem too big to move—must be done without doubting. What are some doubts or fears that hold you back from using your spiritual authority? List at least five.

	Doubts or fears holding you back from using your spiritual authority
1	
2	
3	
4	
5	

Choose one of these doubts or fears. What would it look like to speak in faith in that particular situation even when you feel uncertain?

2. Read 2 Corinthians 10:3–5. How do Paul's words in this passage help you understand the spiritual nature of the battles you face each day? What "fortresses" or thought patterns might God be calling you to speak truth to this week?

You are to do two things when facing a difficulty. One of them is to have a conversation with the mountain itself. The second thing you are to do is talk to God about the mountain. Unfortunately, far too many of us do neither. Instead, we talk to other people about the problem. Then we talk to ourselves about the problem again. If you've done that enough times, you know it doesn't work. Not only does it fail to move mountains but it usually even makes the mountains grow.[3]

3. When you are facing a difficult situation, are you more likely to talk to others about it or speak God's truth directly to it? What would it look like this week to *talk* less about a particular problem you are facing and *speak* more to it in faith?

Far too many Christians waste the authority given to them in their words by using their words unwisely. When facing a mountain, they complain. When battling an issue, they grumble. When going through a trial or difficulty, they may blame or speak negatively. None of those things will enable you to overcome life's mountains. Jesus said that when you or I face a mountain, we are to speak to it in faith, without doubting.[4]

4. Read Proverbs 18:21. Your words carry the weight of life or death. How should this shape the way you speak in the face of hardship? What needs to change in the way you talk about your challenges, your relationships, or your future?

5. Read Joshua 1:6–9. These verses serve as a reminder that courage in life comes from knowing that God is with you. How should this truth empower you to speak boldly in faith, even when your circumstances feel intimidating or uncertain?

Study 3

CLEAR THE BLOCK

There's a reason some prayers feel like they bounce off the ceiling. It's not that God is ignoring you. Rather, something is interfering with the connection. And one thing that often blocks access to the power and presence of God is *unforgiveness*.

Forgiveness isn't easy—but it's essential. Jesus didn't suggest it as a bonus feature of spiritual life. He called it a requirement for those who want to walk in kingdom authority. You can't carry bitterness and expect power. You can't hold on to offense and expect breakthrough. This is not because God is being harsh. It's because His kingdom operates on the principle of mercy. He expects you to pass on the same grace He has extended to you. When you refuse to forgive, you're stepping outside the flow of His grace—and outside the flow of His power.

The enemy thrives in environments of bitterness and resentment. As long as unforgiveness remains rooted in your heart, it grants spiritual access to discouragement, distraction, and even deception. But when you release someone through forgiveness, far from "letting them off the hook," you're allowing God to take full control of the situation. Forgiveness breaks the enemy's grip and restores clarity, peace, and authority in your spiritual life. As Jesus said, "Whenever you stand praying, forgive, if you have anything against anyone, so that your Father who is in heaven will also forgive you for your offenses" (Mark 11:25).

As you consider what might be blocking God's power from flowing into your life, ask the Holy Spirit to bring to mind any person or offense you've been holding on to. Are you still carrying the weight of something you were never meant to bear? What emotions rise when you think about letting go? You don't have to feel ready to forgive. You just have to be willing.

Forgiveness is a decision, not a denial. Take one step this week to clear the block and open the door to freedom, even if that step is simply asking God for help to begin.

I. Jesus laid down the principle that forgiveness is a primary condition for answered prayer. How would you rate the current level of connection you feel with God when you pray?

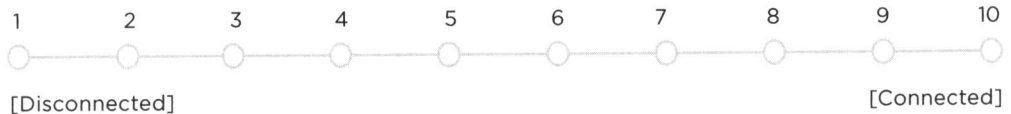

1	2	3	4	5	6	7	8	9	10
O	O	O	O	O	O	O	O	O	O

[Disconnected]   [Connected]

2. Read Ephesians 4:31–32. According to the apostle Paul, forgiveness is both a command and a reflection of what Christ has already done for you. How does remembering the grace you have received help you to release anything you are tempted to hold on to?

The story is told of an elderly wife and husband who went to the doctor because the husband thought his wife was hard of hearing. The doctor asked for an example, so the husband shared how the previous night in the kitchen, he asked his wife what she was cooking. He waited, but there was no answer. So then he decided to move closer, roughly ten feet away, and asked again. Still no answer. Finally he moved right beside her, but still he did not get an answer. When the doctor turned to the wife to ask if she had heard him, she replied, "Yes, of course I heard him—I answered him three times!" Sometimes the problem isn't the *problem*. Or the problem isn't God turning a deaf ear. Or the problem isn't the mountain itself. The problem just may be you needing to increase and expand your faith in God and then speak it out loud.[5]

3. Consider again the current level of connection you feel with God when you pray. Sometimes you might assume God isn't listening when the real issue is

something in your heart—like unforgiveness. How does the story of the husband and wife challenge you to examine whether something in your life might be *blocking* your prayers or spiritual authority? What might need to be cleared for a better connection?

Jesus said, "Blessed are the merciful, for they will receive mercy" (Matthew 5:7). Mercy involves undeserved compassion along with relief from suffering. It is designed to relieve misery and is called upon to forgive or offer a reprieve from negative consequences that you deserve. Mercy is the visible expression of compassion. It's easier to ask for mercy than it is to show it. But Jesus reminded us that we receive mercy from God by showing mercy to others. When it comes time for us to ask for God's mercy in our lives, He checks our mercy account to see what we have done or not done for others. Many people who want mercy are unwilling to give it. But God's blessings are often conditional, and in order to receive mercy, you need to show mercy.[6]

4. Read Luke 6:38. The word "it" in this verse is critical. You are to give the "it" you want to receive. If you want mercy unleashed upon you, it means that you need to give mercy to others. Consider Jesus' words in this verse as you answer the following questions.

> When you consider your need for God's compassion, are there people in your life who need to receive mercy from you? If so, what mercy do you need to extend to them?

What might it cost you to show that mercy? What sacrifice will you need to make?

What might showing mercy to that person or persons unlock in your relationship with God?

5. Read Colossians 3:12–13. Forgiveness isn't based on whether someone deserves it but on what Jesus has already done for you. How does this perspective reshape your view toward someone whom you've struggled to forgive in the past? What might obedience to Christ look like in light of this command?

CATCH UP AND READ AHEAD

Connect with a fellow group member this week and discuss some of the key insights from this session. Use any of the following prompts to guide your discussion.

- What stood out to you most from this session—whether in the group time, personal study, or video teaching? Why do you think it resonated with you?
- Where do you see people today living with spiritual potential but without spiritual power? Have there been times when you've felt "unplugged" from the power of God in your own life?
- In this session, you learned that God's kingdom power is activated through alignment with His rule. How do you respond to the idea that surrender, not striving, is what releases His authority in your life?
- One of the key Scriptures in this week's teaching was Mark 11:22–25, which connects faith, prayer, and forgiveness. How does this passage challenge or reshape the way you think about your prayer life?
- As you look ahead to the rest of the study, what area of kingdom living are you most eager to understand—and why?

Use this time to go back and complete any of the study and reflection questions from previous days that you weren't able to finish. Make a note of any revelations you've had and reflect on any growth or personal insights you've gained.

Read chapter 3 in *Unleashed* before the next group gathering. Make a note of anything in those chapters that stands out to you or encourages you.

BEFORE GROUP MEETING	Read chapter 3 in *Unleashed* Read the Welcome section (page 22)
GROUP MEETING	Discuss the Connect questions Watch the video teaching for session 2 Discuss the questions that follow as a group Do the closing exercise and pray (pages 22–26)
STUDY 1	Complete the personal study (pages 29–31)
STUDY 2	Complete the personal study (pages 32–34)
STUDY 3	Complete the personal study (pages 35–38)
CATCH UP AND READ AHEAD (BEFORE WEEK 3 GROUP MEETING)	Read chapters 4–5 in *Unleashed* Complete any unfinished personal studies (page 39)

CHASING LIFE'S ESSENTIALS

[Pursuit]

*"But seek His kingdom,
and these things will be provided to you."*

LUKE 12:31

WELCOME | READ ON YOUR OWN

In this session, we're going to talk about something that touches all of us: *worry*. Worry keeps us up at night and tags along in our thoughts during the day. Worry doesn't ask for permission. It just shows up—and it often overstays its welcome. Jesus has a word for us concerning worry. He tells us plainly: "Do not worry" (Luke 12:11). And not once, or twice, but over and over again. He tells us not to worry because worry reveals something deeper: a heart that is misaligned with the kingdom.

Worry is what happens when we elevate the urgent over the eternal. But Jesus says, "Seek first the kingdom of God . . . and all these things will be added to you" (Matthew 6:33 ESV). The key to overcoming worry isn't more effort—it's more alignment. When God is in first place, everything else falls into place. When He's not, everything else falls apart. That's why this session is all about kingdom pursuit. We're going to talk about what it means to seek God not *casually* or *occasionally* but *passionately* and *consistently*. Seeking the kingdom isn't about inspiration; it's about order. It's about putting God's rule over every area of our lives: our time, choices, resources, and emotions.

When we make God our first pursuit, something powerful happens. Peace replaces panic. Provision replaces pressure. Clarity replaces confusion. We stop living like spiritual orphans and start living like children who know their Father is near and has already made up His mind to give us the kingdom. So wherever worry has worn you down, get ready. This is your moment to shift, realign, and seek God first. Because when you chase what matters most, you won't have to chase everything else. It'll start chasing you.

CONNECT | 10 MINUTES

If you or any of your group members don't know each other, take a few minutes to introduce yourselves. Then discuss one or both of the following questions:

- What is something that spoke to you in last week's personal study that you would like to share with the group?

  — or —

- When life is overwhelming, what do you do first: pray, plan, panic, or power through? What does that pattern reveal about what you're seeking most?

WATCH | 25 MINUTES

Now watch the video for this session. Below is an outline of the key points covered during the teaching. Record any key concepts that stand out to you.

OUTLINE

I. Worry is concern that has gone out of control.
  A. Worry doesn't ask—it demands. It takes over your thoughts, emotions, and peace.
  B. Jesus says three times in Luke 12, "Do not worry." He's not suggesting it—He's commanding it.
  C. Concern is something you control. Worry is something that starts controlling you.

II. Worry reveals your priorities.
  A. Jesus connects worry to misplaced treasure: "Such is the one who stores up treasure for himself, and is not rich in relation to God" (Luke 12:21).
  B. When your spiritual priorities are out of line, your emotional life will also be out of control.
  C. Worry increases when kingdom perspective decreases because you're living as if your heavenly Father is not in charge.

III. The cure for worry is kingdom pursuit.
  A. Jesus says, "Seek [God's] kingdom, and these things will be provided to you" (Luke 12:31).
  B. *Seeking* means passionate pursuit—placing God's rule first in every decision, every day.
  C. If God isn't first, then He isn't functioning as God in your life. He won't play second string.

IV. God's rule must come before your relief.
  A. You can't claim kingdom power while living outside of kingdom order.
  B. When you skip "first base" with God, nothing else you touch counts.
  C. Once you step into alignment, your Father—who knows what you need—will supply it.

V. You overcome worry by trusting your Father.
  A. Birds don't worry, and they don't have a refrigerator. Lilies don't stress, and they don't have a closet.
  B. When you believe that, you don't have to be ruled by what is trying to knock you down.

VI. The kingdom is not passive. It's power activated by pursuit.
   A. Worry loses its grip when the kingdom takes its place.
   B. Spiritual victory begins when you stop trying to carry it all and start seeking God first.
   C. Like Rocky getting up off the mat, you find new strength when you remember who's in your corner—and who's already won.

NOTES

DISCUSS | 35 MINUTES

Discuss what you just watched by answering the following questions.

1. Read Luke 12:22–24. What does Jesus teach His disciples about God's care through nature? How could remembering this truth help downgrade *worry* to *concern* in your daily life?

2. Jesus said, "Do not keep worrying" (Luke 12:29). What is one area of life where worry has a tendency to take over? What freedom would you gain if you stopped worrying in that area?

3. Read Luke 12:30–31. Jesus ties kingdom-seeking to provision. Why is putting God first the key to overcoming worry? What does "seek His kingdom" look like practically for you?

4. Consider the statement that "worry increases when kingdom perspective decreases." What kinds of things tend to pull your focus away from God's rule and onto earthly concerns?

5. You don't have to live in defeat! You can get up off the mat when worry knocks you down. How could remembering that your Father is in your concern help you in this regard? What would it take for you to trust Him even just a bit more with your worries this week?

RESPOND | 10 MINUTES

In Jesus' day, just as in our own, worry was a common struggle for people. However, Jesus didn't just tell His listeners to *stop* worrying about their needs. Instead, He revealed how they could *replace* worry by seeking something greater: the kingdom of God. Consider this truth as you prayerfully read the following verses and reflect on the questions that follow.

> "And do not seek what you are to eat and what you are to drink, and do not keep worrying. For all these things are what the nations of the world eagerly seek; and your Father knows that you need these things. But seek His kingdom, and these things will be provided to you. Do not be afraid, little flock, because your Father has chosen to give you the kingdom."
>
> **LUKE 12:29–32**

Underline the words or phrases that show how Jesus contrasts worldly worry with kingdom focus. What comfort and/or challenge do you find in these statements?

What is one way you can seek God's kingdom this week instead of seeking control? How could that choice help you respond differently to situations that usually trigger worry in you?

PRAY | 10 MINUTES

As you close this session, take a few minutes to talk to your Father—the One who knows your needs and cares deeply for you. Invite Him to help you trade worry for trust and fear for focus. Thank Him that He hasn't left you to figure it out all alone but has already chosen to give you the kingdom.

PERSONAL STUDY

This week's group time reminded you that worry isn't just a mental burden—it's a spiritual indicator. And the antidote Jesus offers isn't more striving—it's more seeking. You don't overcome anxiety by taking control but by giving God His rightful place as first in your life. When you align with His rule, you experience His peace. The readings in this personal study time will give you the chance to dive deeper into these truths that Jesus taught—truths that speak directly to the stress, fear, and uncertainty that so many of us carry.

Each reading will help you take a closer look at what it means to live free from the grip of worry by living under the covering of God's kingdom. As you reflect, let this be more than a checklist—let it be a conversation. Be open. Be real. Allow space for God to reset your focus, renew your trust, and reframe your everyday choices around His promises. Continue to write down your responses to the questions, as you will be given a few minutes to share your insights in the next session if you are engaging in this study with a group. If you are reading *Unleashed* alongside this study, first review chapter 3 of the book.

Study 1

WHEN WORRY GRADUATES

Worry doesn't arrive all at once. It graduates. One anxious thought builds on another until your heart is overwhelmed, your sleep is disrupted, and your perspective is clouded. Before long, you're living under the weight of something God never intended for you to carry. Jesus speaks directly to this burden in Luke 12:22 when He says, "Do not worry" (verse 22). This is not just advice. It's a line in the sand.

Jesus gives it not because your problems don't matter to your Father but because your Father already knows what you need. He also draws a distinction between concern and worry. Concern is thoughtful, responsible, and drives you to take action. Worry paralyzes you. Concern leads you to pray; worry leads you to panic. Concern keeps you grounded; worry spirals you out of control. The difference isn't just emotional—it's spiritual. It reveals what you believe about God's character.

Jesus states, "Your Father knows that you need these things" (verse 30). That simple phrase pulls back the curtain on why worry is unnecessary. God isn't inattentive or unaware. He's present. He's paying attention. And He's your Father—not just a ruler, not just a rescuer, but a relational provider who cares about what concerns you.

Jesus doesn't dismiss your need for food, clothing, provision, or safety. He simply puts those needs in their proper place. They aren't what you're supposed to seek *first*. God is. "Seek His kingdom," Jesus said, "and these things will be provided to you" (verse 31). When you put God in His rightful place, you're not ignoring your needs but trusting He already sees, already knows, and already has a plan for you.

The opposite of worry isn't apathy but alignment. It's choosing to let the kingdom be your priority and God's presence be your peace. It's remembering that worry doesn't protect your future but steals your peace. When you realign your heart with the truth that God is already at work . . . everything in your life begins to shift. This week, ask yourself: *Where has worry taken the driver's seat?* Consider what it would look like to downgrade that worry back to concern and bring it under kingdom rule.

I. Read Matthew 6:25–30. What does Jesus teach about God's care for creation? How does this speak to your current concerns?

2. What is one specific area in your life where a concern has "graduated" into worry? What has been the emotional or spiritual cost?

> Concern that has graduated into worry:

> What has been the emotional or spiritual cost:

God wants you to pursue His reign and His rule. He wants you to pursue His agenda. He wants you to apply His thinking, His principles, and His approach to every area of your life. Until you do that, you won't be unleashing much of anything good at all. God is not to be used like a spare tire—there if you need it in a desperate situation but ignored and forgotten at all other times. Unfortunately, what many people do is seek God when life goes flat or they hit a bump, but they keep Him in the trunk until the next flat occurs.[7]

3. In what area(s) do you find it hardest to pursue God's reign, rule, and agenda? What would it look like to *actually* apply His thinking, principles, and approach to *every* area of your life?

4. Read Philippians 4:6–7. What does Paul instruct you to do when you feel anxious "about anything"? What practical steps are you taking to replace anxiety with prayer and trust?

Jesus instructed His disciples to seek God's kingdom first in the context of telling them they did not need to worry or be afraid. The entire passage centers on this theme. That tells us that one of the premier benefits of seeking God and His kingdom involves a freedom from worry, stress, and fear. God has given us the formula for living a peace-filled, calm life based on confidence in Him. He's given us the prescription for peace and the antidote to anxiety. We can live a life of peace when we prioritize Christ.[8]

5. Read 1 Peter 5:6–7. Worry often starts with a legitimate concern—but when it begins to control your thoughts, emotions, and decisions, it reveals a deeper issue of trust. What would it look like this week to "cast all your anxiety" on God? How would that demonstrate you are following Jesus' command to seek God's kingdom first in all you do?

Study 2

SEEK FIRST

Jesus didn't say "don't seek" things like food, drink, clothing, and everything else we need. He merely said to seek God's kingdom *first.* The problem isn't that we're seeking—it's that we often seek the wrong things in the wrong order. Most of us wake up chasing what we think we need: security, status, success, affirmation. But Jesus redirects us. "But seek His kingdom, and these things will be provided to you" (Luke 12:31).

This isn't just a positive life tip. It's a reordering of the soul. Seeking God's kingdom first means placing His rule over every other demand. It's not about adding Him to your list—it's about putting Him at the top and letting everything else fall into place beneath His reign.

Jesus links worry to disordered priorities. The more your life is centered on "these things," the more you'll be consumed by fear and lack. But the more you chase God's rule, the more you'll experience His provision and peace.

So, how do we seek the kingdom first? It's not just about church attendance or saying the right prayers. It's about realigning your motives, your decisions, your schedule, and your relationships around God's authority. It's a lifestyle of intentional pursuit. As God says in Jeremiah 29:13, "You will seek Me and find Me when you search for Me with all your heart."

God doesn't play hide-and-seek. He promises to be found when we seek Him *fully,* not partially. That's the key. Many of us seek God when we need Him, but not because we want to know Him. We chase His blessings without surrendering to His rule. The kingdom doesn't work that way. It's all or nothing. First place or no place.

Take inventory this week. What are you seeking first? What's driving your thoughts, your time, your energy? If it's anything other than the kingdom of God, it's time to reorder. The King is not asking for your leftovers—He's inviting you to trust Him with the lead. When you seek Him first, you don't lose anything worth having. You gain everything that matters.

I. Read Matthew 6:31–34. What does Jesus identify as "these things"? What is the promise that Jesus offers about "these things" when you put God first?

2. Read Jeremiah 29:13–14. What does it look like to seek God "with all your heart"—not just for what He can give but for who He is? What would need to shift in you for that to happen?

Anytime God is not first, He is eclipsed by an idol. He will not tolerate that. Just like a run doesn't count if a baseball player fails to step on first base before rounding the bases to home plate, the promises of God's kingdom and His covenantal blessings do not flow to you when you fail to put Him first. All of these blessings and the unleashing of His spiritual authority go out the window when you choose not to place Him first in your life.[9]

3. Turn to Exodus 20:1–3. God tells His people, "You shall have no other gods before Me." While we may not bow to golden statues, we often give first place in our lives to lesser things like success, security, and even our own plans. What is one area where something or someone else has taken priority over God in your life? How do these verses confront that pattern—and what step could you take this week to give God rightful first place again?

God has made it clear you ought to seek His kingdom first, at all times. You are not to allow the kingdom of this culture to prevent you from missing the kingdom of God and His agenda. Rather, you must make a big deal of prioritizing God in your decision-making. When you do that, you receive spiritual benefits—one of them being a reduction in stress and worry.[10]

4. What does it currently look like for you to "make a big deal" of God in your daily decisions? Think about specific areas—your schedule, relationships, finances, and thought life. How might intentionally seeking God's perspective in each area begin to shift your worry levels?

Area	How God's perspective could shift worry levels
Schedule	
Relationships	
Finances	
Thought life	

5. Read Psalm 37:1–5. You are invited to "trust in the LORD" (verse 3), "delight yourself in the LORD" (verse 4), and "commit your way to the LORD" (verse 5). In what situations in life have you been trying to do it all on your own instead of entrusting it to God? How might releasing control and seeking His kingdom first free you from the burden of outcomes?

Study 3

YOUR FATHER KNOWS

When life feels uncertain, it's easy to believe the lie that you're on your own—that everything depends on you. Jesus interrupts such thinking with a powerful truth: "Your Father knows." He says, "All these things are what the nations of the world eagerly seek; and your Father knows that you need these things. But seek His kingdom, and these things will be provided to you. Do not be afraid, little flock, because your Father has chosen to give you the kingdom" (Luke 12:30–32).

This is more than reassurance. It's a redefinition. God is your *Father*—and He's already made up His mind to care for you. When Jesus calls His disciples a "little flock," He is reminding us that we are not forgotten. We belong to a Shepherd who is present and powerful. Worry loses its grip when we believe we are known, seen, and loved by a good Father. And this Father doesn't just respond to our needs but prepares for them: "So if you, despite being evil, know how to give good gifts to your children, how much more will your Father who is in heaven give good things to those who ask Him!" (Matthew 7:11).

Living in this reality reshapes how we pray. We're not approaching a reluctant ruler—we're speaking to a loving Father. When we come to Him in faith, we don't have to convince Him to care. He already does. Trust is not passive—it's active dependence on the character of God. It says, "Even if I don't understand the outcome, I still know the One who holds it." And that knowing changes everything.

Trusting God as your heavenly Father means you don't have to carry what He's already claimed or earn what He's already promised. But that adjustment in mindset requires daily surrender. It means releasing control of the things that are not yours to manage and anchoring your identity not in your performance but in your position—as a child of the King.

So this week, pause and ask yourself: *Where am I living like a spiritual orphan? Where do I need to remember, "My Father knows"?* God is not withholding. He's waiting for you to come close, trust deeply, and rest fully in His care.

1. Reread Matthew 6:32 and compare to Luke 12:30. Where in your life do you feel most tempted to believe you've been forgotten by God? How might Jesus' words in these verses help to remind you of God's fatherly care as you go about your week?

2. Read Isaiah 40:10–11. How does the image of God as a powerful yet tender and attentive Shepherd speak to the pace and pressure you're living under right now? Where might God be inviting you to rest rather than strive?

Not everyone has a good experience with their earthly fathers, so the concept of a good Father may be distant. When Jesus spoke these words, He was referring to the excellent qualities in a father. And while God is supremely God—omnipotent, omniscient, and omnipresent—He is also Daddy. He is also a relational God who desires to be close to you and me. He has all the attributes of a good father: kindness, love, care, provision, empathy, and more. A good father pursues the well-being and development of his child, providing all that is needed to launch his child into adulthood successfully. A good father would never leave his child in a situation where his child would be left to fend for himself. He would not abandon his child in need. Good fathers will often do this even at great personal sacrifice. God, as our good Father, does this as well. And more.[11]

3. When you think about God as your father, do you picture someone who is kind, present, and protective or someone who is distant and uninvolved? How might embracing the truth that God will *never* abandon you—that He will never leave you in a situation where you need to fend for yourself—reshape the way you approach Him in times of need?

If you choose to abandon God's kingdom program in order to allow the culture, secular society, your friends, or even your own thoughts and desires to become your priority, you cannot expect God's favor. You cannot expect God's power. You cannot expect God's divine provision. Just like a good father would not enable his children to continue in drug abuse or supply his children's addictive habits either financially or with the substance itself, God will not enable you in your pursuit of anything other than Him. He will allow you to live a life earmarked by idolatry. But He will not supernaturally supply you with all you need if you are making other things an idol over Him.[12]

4. Read 1 Samuel 15:22–23. The prophet Samuel's words remind us that obedience matters more to God than performance. Sometimes we do good things but avoid God's first-place rule in our lives—striving in one area while withholding surrender in another.

> Where might you be offering "sacrifice" in your spiritual life but neglecting obedience to the Lord?

Has anything—even something good—taken the place of God's full authority in your heart? If so, what is that thing?

What would it mean for you to realign this week by stepping into full obedience, even if it requires letting go of something that's been comfortable but wrongly prioritized?

5. Jesus said, "Do not be afraid, little flock, for your Father has been pleased to give you the kingdom" (Luke 12:32 NIV). What does it mean to you that God is *pleased* to give—not grudgingly or conditionally—the resources and care of His kingdom? In what areas of your life have fear or striving replaced trust in your Father's willingness to provide?

CATCH UP AND READ AHEAD

Connect with a fellow group member this week and discuss some of the key insights from this session. Use any of the following prompts to guide your discussion.

- What insight or truth from this session—whether in the group time, personal study, or video teaching—stuck with you the most? Why do you think it especially struck you at this point in your life?
- Jesus said, "Seek His kingdom, and these things will be provided to you" (Luke 12:31). What are some of the "things" you tend to chase first? How has that order been challenged as you've gone through this session?
- God is not just *Creator*—He is *Father*. How does viewing Him as your provider, protector, and guide shift how you process fear, stress, or decision-making?
- Where have you struggled with worry this week? How could trust in your Father's care free you to rest, release control, or realign with His will?
- As you prepare for the next session, what is one area of your life where you want to seek God's kingdom first—and what might that look like practically?

Use this time to go back and complete any of the study and reflection questions from previous days that you weren't able to finish. Make a note of any revelations you've had and reflect on any growth or personal insights you've gained.

Before next time, catch up on any unfinished personal study sections and read chapters 4–5 in *Unleashed*. Jot down any key takeaways or fresh insights that you have as you continue your journey.

BEFORE GROUP MEETING	Read chapters 4-5 in *Unleashed* Read the Welcome section (page 42)
GROUP MEETING	Discuss the Connect questions Watch the video teaching for session 3 Discuss the questions that follow as a group Do the closing exercise and pray (pages 42–46)
STUDY 1	Complete the personal study (pages 49-52)
STUDY 2	Complete the personal study (pages 53-55)
STUDY 3	Complete the personal study (pages 56-58)
CATCH UP AND READ AHEAD (BEFORE WEEK 4 GROUP MEETING)	Read chapter 6 and 8 in *Unleashed* Complete any unfinished personal studies (page 59)

A LIFE THAT STANDS FIRM

[Commitment + Purpose]

Therefore, since we receive a kingdom which cannot be shaken, let's show gratitude, by which we may offer to God an acceptable service with reverence and awe.

HEBREWS 12:28

WELCOME | READ ON YOUR OWN

In this session, we're stepping into one of the most personal and powerful invitations Jesus ever extended: "Follow Me." Following Jesus isn't about comfort, convenience, or cultural tradition. Rather, it's about surrender and trading our casual affiliations for an all-in, eyes-ahead, no-turning-back kind of faith.

We live in a world that has two kinds of fans. *Cultural* fans show up occasionally. They watch from a distance. *Committed* fans show up all the time. They watch from up close. Jesus, in Luke 9:57–62, encountered three people who were like cultural fans. They wanted to follow Him, but with conditions. One said that he would follow only if it came with comfort. Another delayed, waiting for security. A third hesitated, wanting his family's approval. Jesus didn't rebuke them but clarified what kingdom commitment requires: no delays, no distractions, and no divided loyalties.

When life shakes, as we read in Hebrews 12:28, it's not necessarily *punishment* but *positioning*. God allows what can be shaken to fall away so what is unshakable—His kingdom—remains. When that kingdom becomes our priority, our posture shifts. We stop auditioning Jesus for our plans and start aligning our lives to His mission.

This session is your invitation to move from the sidelines to service. It's not about adding more to your schedule but about rearranging your heart. You were made for more than watching the game. You were called to play your part.

CONNECT | 10 MINUTES

Get this session started by choosing one or both of the following questions to discuss together as a group:

- What is something that spoke to you in last week's personal study that you would like to share with the group?

  — or —

- How do you respond when something in your life gets shaken? What might that reaction reveal about your current level of spiritual commitment?

WATCH | 25 MINUTES

Now watch the video for this session. Below is an outline of the key points covered during the teaching. Record any key concepts that stand out to you.

OUTLINE

I. Commitment reveals the kind of Christian you are.
   A. Just like fans differ in their devotion to a sports team, so Christians vary in their level of commitment.
   B. Cultural Christians show up occasionally. Casual Christians stay when it's easy. But committed Christians are all in—regardless of the cost.
   C. The issue of commitment is a kingdom issue. Only the committed are positioned to experience God's power.

II. Jesus redefines discipleship in Luke 9:57-62.
   A. Three people are interested in following Jesus, but each has a different condition or excuse.
   B. Jesus doesn't lower the bar. He raises it, making clear the kingdom requires full surrender.
   C. Following Jesus means no delays, no distractions, and no divided loyalties.

III. Following Jesus isn't always comfortable.
   A. The first man offers to follow, but Jesus tells him there may not even be a place to sleep.
   B. Commitment isn't built on ease but on a willingness to walk through discomfort.
   C. True discipleship means trading comfort for calling when the two collide.

IV. Delayed obedience is still disobedience.
   A. The second man asks to wait until after his father dies, but Jesus knows that's just a stall.
   B. Some delays sound spiritual but are rooted in a desire for security and convenience.
   C. Jesus calls us to follow *now*, not later, because the kingdom doesn't wait.

V. Looking back disqualifies forward movement
   A. The third man wants to follow, but only after going home to say goodbye.
   B. Jesus sees through it—the man is not just saying goodbye but is seeking his family's approval.
   C. You can't plow a straight line while constantly looking back at what was.

VI. Shaking reveals what's unshakable.
  A. Hebrews 12:28 shows that God uses trials to shake what can be shaken—and expose what can't.
  B. Shaking is often God's way of getting our attention and re-centering priorities.
VII. The kingdom doesn't just bless—it sends.
  A. If God can't use you to serve, He won't entrust you with more.
  B. Many people want the promises of the kingdom without the responsibilities.
  C. The kingdom is bigger than "me, myself, and I." It's about being usable for God.

NOTES

DISCUSS | 35 MINUTES

Discuss what you just watched by answering the following questions.

1. Jesus challenges a man in Luke 9:57–58 who wanted to follow Him but was evidently not willing if it impacted his comfort. What does Jesus' response reveal about the cost of true discipleship? How does this challenge your current view of following Jesus?

2. A second man, in Luke 9:59–60, said he also wanted to follow Jesus but asked to delay his commitment so he could go and bury his father. How did this actually represent a delay that *seemed* reasonable but was actually an *excuse* for not committing fully to Jesus?

3. A third man, in Luke 9:61–62, also asked to delay his commitment to follow Jesus so he could say goodbye to those at home. What does Jesus' response indicate about who is "fit" for the kingdom? Where are you tempted to look back instead of moving forward in faith?

4. God will often "shake" things up in your life not to *punish* you but to *position* you for His kingdom work. When is a specific time in your life that God used a trial, obstacle, or challenge to redirect your focus or priorities? How did you respond to that "shaking"?

5. Think about the three types of Christians discussed in this session: *cultural* Christians, *casual* Christians, and *committed* Christians. Which group would you say that you are in? If you are the *cultural* or *casual* group, how could you move to *committed* in this season of life?

RESPOND | 10 MINUTES

Jesus calls you to respond without delay, without excuses, and without looking back. Commitment isn't proven in comfort; it's revealed in surrender. In fact, God often uses trials and disruptions to "shake loose" the distractions that are keeping you from fully embracing His kingdom. When everything feels unstable, God invites you to build your life on what *cannot* be shaken. Reflect on this as you read the following verses and answer the questions that follow.

> Therefore, since we receive a kingdom which cannot be shaken, let's show gratitude, by which we may offer to God an acceptable service with reverence and awe; for our God is a consuming fire.
>
> **HEBREWS 12:28–29**

According to this passage, receiving an unshakable kingdom from God should lead you to gratitude and service. What might that look like in your current season?

Is there a place in your life where you've been delaying obedience to Christ? What would it mean to say *yes* to Jesus now without waiting for the perfect conditions?

PRAY | 10 MINUTES

As you close, take a few moments to examine your heart. Ask God to reveal any areas where you've been holding back in fully following Him. Acknowledge where you've hesitated, delayed, or looked back. Thank Him for His guidance when life feels uncertain and ask the Holy Spirit to steady your focus, deepen your trust, and strengthen your resolve to serve. End by offering yourself again to God—fully, freely, and without reservation. He is worthy of your *yes*!

PERSONAL STUDY

In this week's group time, you saw Jesus draw a hard line between good intentions and true discipleship. His call isn't to those who want to audit the faith from a safe distance. It's to those willing to go all in, even when it's uncomfortable, inconvenient, or unpopular. The readings in this personal study time will help you reflect on what commitment looks like in real time. You'll examine where hesitation, comfort, or divided focus may be holding you back from fully engaging your purpose. You'll also consider how God sometimes uses trials not to punish but to prepare—to shake loose anything that keeps you from walking in step with His priorities.

Let these reflections guide you deeper. Sit with the questions. Bring your whole self to the process. And ask God to show you what He's calling you to lay down, what He's inviting you to pick up, and how He wants to strengthen your commitment to live for something that lasts. Continue to write down your responses to the questions, as you will be given a few minutes to share your insights in the next session if you are engaging in this study with a group. If you are reading *Unleashed* alongside this study, first review chapters 4–5 of the book.

Study 1

THE COST OF COMMITMENT

"Blessed is the one who trusts in the Lord, whose confidence is in him" (Jeremiah 17:7 NIV). Everybody wants the blessings. Not everybody wants the burden. That's why when a man came up to Jesus and said that he would follow Him wherever He went, Jesus didn't pat him on the back and say, "That's great—let's go."

Instead, Jesus gave him a dose of kingdom reality. "The foxes have holes," He said, "and the birds of the sky have nests, but the Son of Man has nowhere to lay His head" (Luke 9:58). In other words, Jesus said to the man, "Are you sure you know what you're signing up for?" A lot of people want to be near Jesus for what they can *get*. They want the miracles, the feel-good moments, the blessing—but they don't want the bruises. They want the crown but are not interested in carrying the cross.

Jesus wasn't trying to run the man off. He was being honest with him, because kingdom commitment doesn't come with a comfort guarantee. There is no promise of padded pews and smooth paths. In fact, Jesus was letting the man know that following Him might mean that he didn't even know where he would be sleeping that night. We've got too many Christians today who want a convenient Jesus. They'll serve—if it fits their schedule. They'll give—if there's enough left over. They'll go to church—as long as nothing else comes up. Jesus isn't looking for convenience. He's looking for commitment.

Discipleship is not about adding Jesus to our agenda. It's about surrendering our whole lives to His rule. It's not just saying "I'll follow You" with our lips but also showing it with our steps, even when the path gets rocky. But here's the clincher: When we follow Jesus fully, we get more than a temporary blessing. We get His presence . . . and His presence is what gives us peace when things go left. His presence is what gives us power when life gets hard. His presence is what makes the sacrifice worth it.

Don't follow Jesus for the perks. Follow Him for the purpose. Follow Him because He is King. And when He calls you to follow, don't ask where He's going—just go. Because wherever Jesus leads, it's better than staying comfortable without Him.

1. Read Philippians 3:7–8. Paul says he counts all things as "loss" compared to knowing Christ. What would it look like for you to adopt that mindset in an area of your life today?

2. Where in your faith journey have you found yourself expecting convenience from God instead of surrendering to His direction—no matter the cost?

"Then a scribe came and said to Him, 'Teacher, I will follow You wherever You go.' And Jesus said to him, 'The foxes have holes and the birds of the sky have nests, but the Son of Man has nowhere to lay His head'" (Matthew 8:19–20). Jesus' words to this scribe are for us as well. Are we following Jesus because of our love for Jesus, or do we come to church and read our Bible for the kingdom goodies He offers? Sure, there are benefits to following Jesus, but Jesus wants to be sure we are also game for the difficulties. God is not looking for gold diggers. A lot of people hang out with God for His goodies. They will praise God in hopes of His provision. But when things go south, they simply slip away. They do not proclaim like Job, "Though He slay me, I will hope in Him. Nevertheless I will argue my ways before Him" (Job 13:15).[13]

3. Turn to Habakkuk 3:17–19. When circumstances get hard, do you pull away from God or press in with honest trust? What would it take to follow God with resilient hope and love—even when life doesn't go the way you expected?

4. Read Matthew 16:24–25 and Galatians 2:20. Each of these verses describe the cost of discipleship. Jesus calls us to take up our cross—and Paul says his life is no longer his own.

What do you think it means to "take up [your] cross" (Matthew 16:24)?

What do you think it means to be "crucified with Christ" (Galatians 2:20)?

How do these verses challenge your understanding of surrender?

What might need to die in you so Christ can fully live through you?

Losing your life for the sake of Christ is what it takes to unleash the kingdom power of God in all you do. Following Jesus is no small thing. It's not a hobby. It's not a side hustle. Following Jesus involves a heartfelt, dedicated commitment to Him and what He says to do at all times. Far too many Christians think following Jesus is like going to an ice cream social. It's all fun and games. It's one big party. But an ice cream social is not real life. Just like the Magic Kingdom is not real life. There is one kingdom that is real; that is God's kingdom, and it's not a cotton-candy experience.[14]

5. Read 2 Timothy 3:12 and John 16:33. When have you tried to take the easy path in following Jesus? How might a deeper understanding of perseverance reshape the way you walk with Him through hardship?

Study 2

DROP THE DELAY

There's something about a delayed response that feels safe. "Let me get through this season." "Let me figure a few things out first." "Let me make sure it won't cost too much." That's where a lot of believers live: between conviction and convenience.

When Jesus called one man to follow Him, he replied, "Lord, permit me first to go and bury my father" (Luke 9:59). This sounds noble—even responsible. But most scholars agree that the man's father hadn't yet died. What the man really meant was, "Let me take care of my personal affairs first. When the timing is better, then I'm in."

Jesus responded with urgency: "Allow the dead to bury their own dead; but as for you, go and proclaim everywhere the kingdom of God" (verse 60). Jesus was not being cold. He was making a kingdom point: *Delayed obedience is disobedience.*

It's not that God doesn't understand your responsibilities. It's that He knows the longer you delay, the harder it becomes to say yes. Excuses get more comfortable. The urgency fades—and with it, the clarity of His call. Paul wrote, "Be careful how you walk, not as unwise people but as wise, making the most of your time, because the days are evil" (Ephesians 5:15-16). Time is precious, so following Jesus can't wait for the perfect window. The call to follow is always *now*. Not next month, or when your schedule opens up, or after the stress dies down.

The kingdom doesn't move on your timeline—and God's purposes don't wait for ideal conditions. "If you are willing and obedient, you will eat the good things of the land;" (Isaiah 1:19 NIV). The fruit comes after the follow—not before it. When you delay, you're not just pausing a task but postponing transformation. You're putting distance between God's prompting and your obedience. In that space, faith starts to cool.

So, what have you been putting off? Maybe it's a conversation you know God's been nudging you to have. Maybe it's a step of service you keep pushing to "someday." Whatever it is, don't wait for ease. Don't wait for approval. Don't wait for things to settle down. Jesus isn't asking you to have all the answers. He's asking you to say yes—*now*. Your surrender doesn't need to be perfect. It just needs to be real.

1. Read Ephesians 5:13–16. What does Paul mean when he says to "awake" from slumber? In what areas of life might you be "slumbering" right now?

2. Think about those areas of life that feel "on hold" spiritually for you right now. What is one step of obedience that God has been prompting you to take but you've been delaying? What is keeping you from saying *yes* to Him today?

Dotting the *i*'s and crossing the *t*'s should never come before following Christ. Following Jesus comes with faith. When Jesus asks you to follow Him, He's asking you to follow Him *now*. Jesus knew that in order for the second man to follow Him, he had to have his priorities straight or he would bail out when things got hard. This reflects the conditional commitment so many people have. They will follow Jesus as long as they get what they want. Jesus' point is that the kingdom can't wait, so stop postponing discipleship.[15]

3. Read Proverbs 3:5–6. What conditions have you placed on your obedience to Jesus that are keeping you from trusting Him "with all your heart"? What would it look like to surrender those today and follow Him without delay?

When it comes to following Jesus Christ and advancing His kingdom agenda, you need to make up your mind and keep moving forward. There's no time to recapture the good ol' days. Discipleship is a commitment that leaves all else behind. You must make yourself fit for the kingdom. You must avail yourself as someone whom God can use. Because if you're still in love with yesterday, then following God is not part of your story.[16]

4. Read James 1:5–8. Are there areas in your life where indecision or attachment to the past is keeping you from moving forward with God? Do you need His wisdom on how to move forward? In the space below, write down the instructions that James provides on this.

But if any of you _____ _____, let him _____ ___ ____ (verse 5).

But he must _____ __ _____, without any _____ (verse 6a).

That person ought ___ __ _____ that he will receive _____ from the Lord, being a _____-_____ man, _____ in all his ways (verses 7–8).

What would it take for you to release yesterday and follow after Jesus with full focus today?

5. Looking back over this session, where have you sensed God inviting you into deeper obedience but you've been slow to respond? What might shift in your life if you trusted Him enough to act *today* instead of waiting for a more convenient *tomorrow*?

ROOTED IN THE STORM

Life has a way of shaking us to the core. Unexpected loss. Lingering uncertainty. Doors that close. Plans that unravel. In those moments, when everything feels unstable, the question isn't *if* you'll be shaken but *what* will remain.

The author of Hebrews speaks directly to this kind of "shaking" in life. He tells us that God allows shaking not to *destroy* us but to *reveal* what is truly unshakable: "Therefore, since we receive a kingdom which cannot be shaken, let's show gratitude" (12:28). In other words, when life shakes, God's kingdom stays steady. And those who are kingdom grounded—anchored in His rule, purpose, and truth—are the ones who remain still standing when the dust settles.

Shaking strips away our illusions of control. It exposes our false anchors like comfort, security, reputation, or routine. And shaking invites us into something deeper—a life that doesn't just believe in God's kingdom but also lives from it. This is the kind of life that doesn't get uprooted by every hard season or emotional storm. It stands firm because it is rooted in something stronger than circumstance.

But make no mistake—being rooted in the storm doesn't mean you won't feel the wind. It means you've planted your hope where the ground doesn't give way. God's kingdom isn't a backup plan for when yours falls apart. It's the *only* plan that was never meant to. And when your roots go deep, your fruit can still grow. Gratitude still flows. Purpose still leads. Service still happens—not because things are easy but because you are tethered to something eternal.

If you're in a season where everything feels like it's shaking, the challenge today is to not just ask God to stop the storm but ask Him to help you go deeper through it. Ask Him to remove what doesn't belong so what is eternal can remain. Ask Him to make you kingdom grounded so that no matter what happens, lightning strikes and all, you'll still be standing tall.

This isn't a call to spiritual toughness. It's a call to spiritual surrender. The deeper your roots in His kingdom, the steadier your soul will be in the chaos.

1. How do you typically react when life feels unsure or unstable? Use the scales below to indicate how you tend to respond in each of the following areas of life.

How do you respond when your financial situation is shaken?

1	2	3	4	5	6	7	8	9	10

[Total panic]   [Some trust in God]   [Total trust in God]

How do you respond when your future plans are shaken?

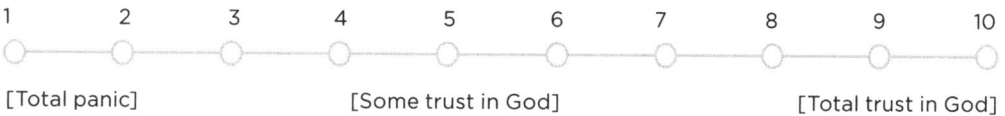

1	2	3	4	5	6	7	8	9	10

[Total panic]   [Some trust in God]   [Total trust in God]

How do you respond when your friendships and relationships are shaken?

1	2	3	4	5	6	7	8	9	10

[Total panic]   [Some trust in God]   [Total trust in God]

2. Read Hebrews 12:26–29. How would you define the "things which can be shaken" in your life? How would you define or describe those things "which cannot be shaken"?

God will either allow or create turbulent times in our lives and circumstances in order to get our attention. He will do this so that we will listen attentively to Him. If we are too busy having fun watching movies, playing video games, or listening to music that we tune Him out when He speaks, He knows how to make us listen. He knows how to shift our focus from whatever it was on back to Him. Thus, rather than getting mad at God, get glad. He allows these disturbances to get you back on track.[17]

3. Think about a time when God used a disruption to get your attention. How did that moment change your direction? What did God "shake loose" in your life through that disruption?

If an earthquake happened while an airplane flew over it in the sky, no one in the plane would feel the earthquake. That's because the plane would not be attached to land in any way. It's the things that are attached that get shaken in an earthquake. What God wants to do is lift you up to a new spiritual reality of a kingdom that is not attached to this world. He doesn't want you to get "shook up" when this world experiences the chaos it frequently does. When you attach yourself to God and His kingdom, you will withstand the challenges of this world because you will have unleashed His rule within you. Your connection to God stabilizes you because His kingdom cannot be shaken.[18]

4. Read Colossians 3:1–4. What does Paul say that you should "keep seeking"? In what areas are you still too attached to what's shakable? How would shifting your mindset to God's unshakable kingdom give you greater peace and stability during uncertain seasons?

5. Turn to Revelation 3:15–16. Where in your life has God revealed areas of "lukewarm" commitment, delayed obedience, or misplaced focus? What is one step you can take today to follow Him with deeper surrender in those areas?

CATCH UP AND READ AHEAD

Connect with a fellow group member this week and discuss some of the key insights from this session. Use any of the following prompts to guide your discussion.

- This session highlighted the difference between interest and commitment. What part of Jesus' call to follow challenged you the most—and why?
- You explored how delayed obedience often hides behind good intentions. What's something God might be asking you to do now—not later?
- Hebrews 12:28 reminds us that God allows shaking to reveal what is unshakable. What did you identify about how you typically respond when life feels unstable? How has your perspective on trials shifted this week?
- It is critical to follow after Jesus without conditions or divided priorities. What are some of the common distractions that keep believers from going "all in"? How do you fight those in your own life?
- As you prepare for the next session, what is one personal takeaway you want to hold onto—and one area you want to keep growing in?

Take this opportunity to revisit any unfinished study or reflection questions from previous days that you weren't able to finish. As you review, jot down any fresh insights, breakthroughs, or areas of growth you've noticed along the way.

Read chapters 6 and 8 in *Unleashed* before the next group gathering. Make a note of anything in those chapters that stands out to you or encourages you.

BEFORE GROUP MEETING	Read chapters 6 and 8 in *Unleashed* Read the Welcome section (page 62)
GROUP MEETING	Discuss the Connect questions Watch the video teaching for session 4 Discuss the questions that follow as a group Do the closing exercise and pray (pages 62–66)
STUDY 1	Complete the personal study (pages 69–71)
STUDY 2	Complete the personal study (pages 72–75)
STUDY 3	Complete the personal study (pages 76–78)
CATCH UP AND READ AHEAD (BEFORE WEEK 5 GROUP MEETING)	Read chapters 7 and 9 in *Unleashed* Complete any unfinished personal studies (page 79)

Session Four

WHAT MATTERS MOST

[Truth + Mysteries]

"But the one sown with seed on the good soil, this is the one who hears the word and understands it, who indeed bears fruit and produces, some a hundred, some sixty, and some thirty times as much."

MATTHEW 13:23

WELCOME | READ ON YOUR OWN

We live in a world that confuses truth with opinion—and the consequences show up in every area of life. The absence of truth isn't just a cultural problem. It's a spiritual one. When we drift from God's Word, we lose access to the power, peace, and perspective He longs to give. Jesus made it clear that His kingdom operates by truth—not by trends, feelings, or public opinion. Truth isn't an option. It's the standard by which reality is measured. Until we anchor our lives in what God says is true, we'll always be flying coach—barely getting by instead of living in the fullness He offers.

Jesus told a parable in Luke 8:4-15 in which He described four kinds of soil—four heart conditions that determine how people receive God's Word. Some reject it outright. Some receive it with excitement but it doesn't take root. Some get distracted. But one kind of soil bears lasting fruit: the heart that clings to truth and lives it out with perseverance. The goal of this session is to help you become that kind of soil. A truth-filled life isn't just informed but also transformed. And the more you abide in God's Word, the more you'll see His power released in your everyday life.

The question isn't whether God is speaking to you. The question is whether you are *rooted* enough in His Word to receive it. If you're tired of spiritual turbulence and long for a deeper experience of God's kingdom, it's time to bump up to first class. Not by striving but by soaking. Not by doing more but by holding fast to truth until it shapes everything about your journey. Let's dive in!

CONNECT | 10 MINUTES

Get this session started by choosing one or both of the following questions to discuss together as a group:

- What is something that spoke to you in last week's personal study that you would like to share with the group?

  — *or* —

- When was a time a truth from God's Word brought clarity in a difficult situation? How did that truth change the way you responded or saw things?

WATCH | 25 MINUTES

Now watch the video for this session. Below is an outline of the key points covered during the teaching. Record any key concepts that stand out to you.

OUTLINE

I. The kingdom journey looks different depending on your relationship with truth.
   A. All believers in Christ are headed to heaven, but not all travel with the same spiritual experience.
   B. Without truth, the journey is marked by turbulence, not transformation.
   C. Jesus teaches in John 8:31–32 that abiding in His Word leads to knowing the truth—and that truth is what sets us free for the journey ahead.

II. God's truth is the seed, but the soil determines the harvest.
   A. The Word of God is always powerful, but its impact depends on the condition of the heart.
   B. Jesus said in the parable of the soils that some seed (God's Word) falls beside the road. The devil takes it away from people so they won't believe (Luke 8:12).
   C. If Satan can keep truth from taking root, he can keep lives from being transformed.
   D. A hardened heart leaves the field exposed to theft and the seed never has a chance to grow.

III. Shallow soil won't sustain deep roots.
   A. Jesus described rocky soil as those people who receive the Word with joy, but when testing comes they fall away because they have no firm root (Luke 8:13).
   B. Satan's deception here isn't rejection but shallowness. He's content with a surface response that never leads to lasting change.
   C. God's Word is meant to reach the spirit and reshape the soul. Rocky ground blocks the process.
   D. Without depth, faith will collapse under pressure.

IV. Weeds grow fast and choke out fruit.
   A. Jesus said that thorny soil allows the Word to grow for a time, but it's choked by the cares, riches, and pleasures of life (Luke 8:14).
   B. The enemy doesn't always need to destroy the seed—just distract the soil.
   C. When eternity is eclipsed by urgency, fruit stops forming.
   D. A crowded field looks alive but is overrun and unable to yield what matters most.

V. Good soil is cultivated with perseverance.
  A. Jesus described the good soil as those who hear the word, hold it fast in an honest and good heart, and bear fruit with perseverance (see Luke 8:15).
  B. Satan can't steal this seed, but he still tries to wear down the grower.
  C. Good soil doesn't just happen—it's turned, cleared, watered, and guarded.
  D. When God's truth goes deep and stays long, it produces visible, lasting fruit that blesses others and glorifies Him.

NOTES

DISCUSS | 35 MINUTES

Discuss what you just watched by answering the following questions.

1. Read Luke 8:5–8. Notice in this parable from Jesus that the same seed produces different results depending on the soil. Which type of soil do you most identify with right now? Why?

2. The enemy doesn't always *remove* the seed that God sows—sometimes he just clutters the field. Where in your life might worries be threatening to choke out the Word?

3. Read Galatians 6:7–9. What encouragement do you find in this passage as it relates to "sowing" and "reaping"? How does this reshape the way you view spiritual perseverance?

4. Read James 1:21–22. What does it mean to be good soil? What stands out to you in this passage about the connection between receiving the Word and responding to it?

5. Jesus said the good-soil heart hears the Word, holds fast to it, and perseveres to bear good fruit for God's kingdom. Where do you see signs of good fruit growing in your life right now? Where might God be inviting you to cultivate the soil more intentionally?

RESPOND | 10 MINUTES

Jesus told the parable of the soils to invite honest evaluation. What kind of soil are we? Is the Word bouncing off a hardened heart, getting lost in shallow enthusiasm, or ending up tangled in distractions? Is it going deep enough to produce lasting fruit? Spiritual fruit doesn't grow by accident but comes from soil that has been prepared, protected, and persevered in. Consider these truths as you read the following verse with a listening heart—not just to understand but also to receive. Use the questions that follow to further guide your reflection.

> "But the seed in the good soil—these are the ones who have heard the word with a good and virtuous heart, and hold it firmly, and produce fruit with perseverance."

> **LUKE 8:15**

Search your heart. Is there an area of your life where God's Word has been planted but is not producing anything? If so, what might be blocking its growth?

What is one way you can cultivate "good soil" this week—whether by removing distractions, deepening your root system, or acting on what God has already said?

PRAY | 10 MINUTES

God doesn't scatter His Word aimlessly but plants it with purpose. So, as you wrap up this session, respond to Him not just with your thoughts but also with your trust. Ask Him to help you see where growth has stalled and the roots need to go deeper. Tell Him you're willing to clear out whatever is choking the fruit He's trying to grow in you. As you pray, remember that He's a faithful gardener. If you let Him work the soil, He will bring the harvest.

PERSONAL STUDY

The parable of the soils that you discussed during this week's group time isn't really about farming but about fruitfulness. It's about how the same Word of God can fall on four different types of hearts and only produce growth in one. The readings in this week's personal study will further invite you to examine the condition of your "soil"—not just what you believe about truth but also how much room you've made for it to take root. You'll look at what chokes it out, what keeps it shallow, and what helps it go deep enough to transform your entire life.

You'll also see how Satan doesn't always need to steal the Word—sometimes he just distracts you from it. Whether through worries, worldly pleasures, or shallow living, he works to keep God's truth from bearing fruit. So, take your time in exploring God's Word this week. Ask hard questions. Let the Spirit reveal where the seed has been falling and fruit is waiting to grow. Remember that God has already given the Word . . . and the next move is yours. Also, as you work through these exercises, continue writing down your responses to the questions, as you will be given a few minutes to share your insights at the start of the next session. If you are reading *Unleashed* alongside this study, first review chapters 6 and 8 of the book.

Study 1

TRUTH DOESN'T BEND

In a world that changes its definitions daily, it can be tempting to treat truth like clay—something we shape to fit our preferences. But the truth of God doesn't flex. It doesn't sway with culture, sentiment, or public opinion. It stands firm because it is rooted in the unchanging character of God Himself.

Truth isn't just an idea; it's also a person. Jesus said, "Sanctify them in the truth; Your word is truth" (John 17:17). In that prayer, Jesus didn't ask the Father to make His followers more relevant, more comfortable, or more liked. He asked that they would be set apart—made holy—by truth. His truth. God's truth. The only truth.

When we detach from that standard, we drift. We might still go to church, read devotionals, or try to be "good people," but if our view of truth is soft, our foundation is unstable. Isaiah warns us what happens when society loses its grip on reality: "Woe to those who call evil good, and good evil; who substitute darkness for light and light for darkness; who substitute bitter for sweet and sweet for bitter!" (5:20).

That's not just poetic language—it's a picture of moral and spiritual collapse where lines are blurred and the idea of an absolute right or wrong is labeled intolerant. God's kingdom is built on clarity. As kingdom people, we are called not just to know the truth but to stand in it—even when it's costly, uncomfortable, or unpopular.

Standing in truth means being anchored. It means that when you're tempted to soften God's Word to avoid rejection, or are pressured to compromise for convenience, you remember who authored the words of Scripture and choose obedience over approval. You do this because you recognize truth isn't up for negotiation—and that bending it just bends you. Truth liberates, but it also divides. It has always done both. Jesus didn't water it down for the crowds, and He didn't rewrite it for the critics. He simply spoke what was true and let the seed fall where it would.

This week, take a close look at your internal compass. Are there areas where you've let culture, fear, or comfort reshape what you believe? Where do you need to realign with God's definition of truth? Because truth doesn't bend—and neither should you.

I. On a scale of 1-10, how firmly would you say your life is currently aligned with God's truth—not just in belief but also in practice?

1	2	3	4	5	6	7	8	9	10

[not aligned]   [very aligned]

2. Read Proverbs 30:5-6. What do these verses reveal about the reliability of God's truth and your response to it? Where in your life are you tempted to seek shelter elsewhere?

Truth is defined as the absolute standard by which reality is measured. Truth is God's view on any subject. The reason why this is the case is because God alone is perfect. Perfection can't make a mistake on any subject or else it's no longer perfect. Whenever you disagree with God, you're wrong. Whenever your social circle disagrees with God, they are wrong. Whenever your professor, pastor, or boss disagrees with God, they are wrong. Whenever the politicians disagree with God, they are wrong. There exist two answers to every question: God's and everyone else's. When everyone else disagrees with God, they are wrong. Truth exists as an absolute standard.[19]

3. Turn to Isaiah 5:20-21. What "woe" does Isaiah proclaim? Where in your life are you most tempted to bend truth to fit comfort, culture, or consensus?

4. When truth challenges your preferences or disrupts your plans, how do you typically respond? Consider each of the following questions in your response.

> Do you resist, delay, reinterpret, or surrender? What does that pattern reveal about your trust in God's authority and His right to define reality in your life?

> Are there specific areas where you've been holding onto your version of truth instead of yielding to His? If so, what are those specific areas?

> What might change in your life if you fully surrendered to what God says, even when it's hard?

No doubt Jesus chose the term *seed* in His parable because it provides an easily understandable physical illustration of a spiritual truth. The seed is the life-giving force in order to birth a new reality. It's designed to penetrate the soil of the heart and spirit in order to produce a new life of spiritual maturity. But the seed of the Word of God must also be able to penetrate the soil of our spirit to produce its new life.[20]

5. Read 1 Peter 1:22–23. What is the nature of the seed planted in your heart? What do you need to do to create an environment where God's Word can take root and thrive?

Study 2

GROWTH STARTS BELOW

We live in a culture that prizes the visible. We measure success by what people can see—platforms, titles, results. But in God's kingdom, the most important growth is the kind no one sees at first. Roots always come before fruit. Strength is developed in the soil, not on the stage. And until the Word of God goes deep, it won't last.

In the parable of the soils, the seed sprang up quickly in the rocky soil but then withered just as fast. Why? Because it had no root. "They believe for a while, and in a time of temptation they fall away" (Luke 8:13). That kind of faith isn't fake—it's fragile. It never has a chance to grow beneath the surface. Real growth starts underground. It's where your faith learns to cling in the dark, where conviction is shaped, and where your soul learns to depend on truth. It's also where Satan wages war. If he can't stop you from hearing the Word, he'll try to keep it from settling in. He'll fill your life with noise. He'll tempt you to keep moving fast, staying shallow, and living off borrowed belief. He knows if that Word ever goes deep, he's in trouble.

That's why your private obedience matters more than your public image. Reading the Bible without ever letting it change you is like admiring seeds and never planting them. You can't microwave maturity. There are no shortcuts to depth. You have to let the Word settle in. You have to let it touch the parts of you that are still afraid, still hurting, and still hiding. And you have to do it again tomorrow.

Paul says you are to be "rooted and grounded in love" (Ephesians 3:17). Roots don't grow once and then stop. They deepen over time. In your life, this is done through repetition, resistance, and relationship. The more your roots stretch into God's truth, the more your life can withstand the storms above.

You may feel like not much is happening right now. Maybe you're in a quiet season, a painful one, or one where growth feels invisible. Don't panic. Don't dig up what God is planting. Let the Word go deep. When growth happens below the surface, fruit will follow above it. You weren't made to wilt. You were made to be rooted.

1. Read Jeremiah 17:7–8. What does it mean to be rooted in God? What contrasts do you see between someone who is deeply rooted and someone who is not?

2. When have you sensed God was growing something in you that others couldn't see? How did that hidden growth eventually lead to visible fruit?

Many people today operate solely on the facts they know. All the while, they miss the greater truth that could position them for a greater experience of life. Without truth, many people try to solve issues without getting to the root of the issue itself. They try to mask their pain with pain medication, not realizing there is a deeper source of the pain that needs to be addressed. Truth always goes deeper than facts, and how you approach whatever situation you are facing ought to be reliant on truth, not only on the facts you know.[21]

3. Read Psalm 51:6–7. How do these words reinforce the call to seek truth in the hidden, inward places of your life? As you look at your "innermost being," where might God be calling you to dig deeper beyond surface-level fixes?

The living spirit left unattended will not grow on its own. It must have the seed of the Word of God (the nourishment) to grow. Not only that, but it must also have the right environment (the good soil) to grow as well. The condition of the soul and the receptivity to the Word of God will determine the expansion of new life into maturity. Both will determine how much of God's will, power, and favor you unleash in your life.[22]

4. Turn to Hosea 10:12. Consider these questions as they relate to this verse.

> What does this verse suggest about preparing your heart like soil?

> What would it look like to make space for God's Word to take root in your current season?

What areas of your spiritual life have remained "unattended"?

What needs to shift in your environment or habits to foster deeper growth?

5. Read Colossians 2:6–7. What roles do consistency and foundation play in your spiritual maturity? Where do you sense God inviting you to grow deeper rather than wider right now—and how will you respond to that invitation?

LET IT TAKE ROOT

We often think the hardest part of spiritual growth is *hearing* from God. But more often, the real challenge is *holding on* to what He's already said.

In the parable of the soils, Jesus describes the good soil as those who "have heard the word with a good and virtuous heart, and hold it firmly, and produce fruit with perseverance" (Luke 8:15). Notice that the result—the fruit—comes not just from hearing the Word but also from holding it. Deeply. Repeatedly. Through difficulty, delay, and disappointment. The Word only becomes fruitful when it's rooted.

We all love the idea of breakthrough. We pray for change. But we don't always realize that transformation doesn't come from hearing a truth once but from staying with it. This means resisting the urge to move on too quickly. It means holding onto truth when it doesn't yet feel true in your circumstances. It requires *perseverance*.

But perseverance is where the weeds start to show up. Satan is not concerned if you hear a powerful sermon or open your Bible for five minutes. What threatens him is when the Word lingers in your being—when it starts to shape your thoughts, rewire your responses, and redirect your decisions. That's why he uses pressure, distraction, and delay to try to pry the Word loose before it embeds itself into your life.

Allowing the Word to take root isn't a passive process. It's an active choice to cultivate the ground of your heart. It's a deliberate decision to return to what God said yesterday when you're tempted to quit. James writes that you are to receive the "word implanted" (1:21), like a seed pushed into your soul—not sitting on top but worked in deep enough to take hold. It won't always be comfortable. Growth never is.

Scripture is not intended to be like a sticky note—something to glance at and discard. Rather, God's Word is meant to be a mirror. It's meant to show you where we've misaligned, call you to correction, and remind you of your identity. You don't just glance at it and walk away. You stare until it sticks. You can't bear lasting fruit if you don't let the root go deep. This is where faith becomes more than belief—it becomes endurance. It's where knowing turns into transformation. Let it take root.

I. Read Jesus' explanation of the parable of the sower in Luke 8:11–15. As a reminder, write down what each type of soil represents when it comes to receiving God's Word.

Type of soil	Type of heart this soil represents
verse 12	
verse 13	
verse 14	
verse 15	

2. Read Hebrews 10:23–25. What does it look like for you to "hold firmly" to God's Word in a current area of uncertainty? Where is perseverance being tested in your life right now?

Hearing God's Word and applying God's Word are two vastly different things. It is in the application of the Word of God that the unleashing of the power of God takes place. Applying truth principles to your decisions matters. Applying God's rules to your life makes all the difference. Simply showing up at church to hear a sermon will do nothing for you unless you receive the truth and apply it. Just like receiving a prescription from your doctor will not help you if you do not take the medication as directed, receiving God's Word without applying it produces no results. It is the application of truth that unleashes you to experience your greatest spiritual self.[23]

3. What is an area in your life where you've heard God's Word but haven't applied it? What's holding you back from moving from information to transformation?

The only soil that produces growth in Jesus' parable is the good soil. Jesus explained, "But the seed in the good soil, these are the ones who have heard the word with a good and virtuous heart, and hold it firmly, and produce fruit with perseverance" (Luke 8:15). The good soil includes an honest and good heart. This starts by being honest with *God*. You need to get real and raw with the Lord. He knows the truth anyhow. You might as well admit to Him how you feel, where you struggle, and in what ways you need His help the most.[24]

4. The mercy you receive from God is connected to the mercy you extend to others (see Matthew 5:7). When you consider your need for God's compassion, are there people in your life who need to receive it from you? What might it cost to show them mercy—and what might it unlock in your relationship with God?

5. Read James 1:23–25. How do these verses challenge your current response to God's truth? Where might God be asking you to stop glancing at His Word and start living it?

CATCH UP AND READ AHEAD

Connect with a fellow group member this week and discuss some of the key insights from this session. Use any of the following prompts to guide your discussion.

- What part of this session gave you a fresh perspective on your own walk with God? How did it shift your understanding of spiritual growth?
- Can you think of a time when you knew what God had said but struggled to hold onto it? What helped—or hindered—you in staying rooted?
- You explored the connection between having deep roots and bearing lasting fruit. How have you seen that play out in someone's life—or in your own?
- In what ways do you see the enemy trying to distract, distort, or discourage believers from letting God's Word settle deep?
- As you continue in this study, where do you sense God inviting you to dig deeper rather than move faster—and what might it look like to respond?

Use this time to go back and complete any of the study and reflection questions from previous days that you weren't able to finish. Make a note of any revelations you've had and reflect on any growth or personal insights you've gained.

Read chapter 7 and 9 in *Unleashed* before the next group gathering. Make a note of anything in those chapters that stands out to you or encourages you.

BEFORE GROUP MEETING	Read chapters 7 and 9 in *Unleashed* Read the Welcome section (page 82)
GROUP MEETING	Discuss the Connect questions Watch the video teaching for session 5 Discuss the questions that follow as a group Do the closing exercise and pray (pages 82–86)
STUDY 1	Complete the personal study (pages 89–91)
STUDY 2	Complete the personal study (pages 92–94)
STUDY 3	Complete the personal study (pages 95–98)
CATCH UP AND READ AHEAD (BEFORE WEEK 6 GROUP MEETING)	Read chapter 10 in *Unleashed* Complete any unfinished personal studies (page 99)

LIVING IN ABUNDANCE

[Provision + Blessings]

The earth is the LORD'S,
and all it contains, the world,
and those who live in it.
For He has founded it upon the seas and
established it upon the rivers.

PSALM 24:1-2

WELCOME | READ ON YOUR OWN

We often talk about trusting God with our lives, but many of us live like we're in the driver's seat. We map the route, set the speed, and hope God signs off on our plans. When we live that way, we miss the heart of the kingdom. Because in God's kingdom, He's not the passenger or the co-pilot . . . He's the *conductor*.

Everything changes when we let Him lead. So, in this session, we'll explore what it means to live with a kingdom mindset—not as owners but as stewards. We don't own our breath, our bank accounts, or even our talents. Everything we have is a resource, but God alone is the source. And when we stop confusing the two, we open the door to real abundance—not just in what we receive but also in how we live.

Scripture makes this truth clear. In 1 Chronicles 29:11–12, King David prayed, "Yours is the dominion, Lord, and You exalt Yourself as head over all. Both riches and honor come from You, and You rule over all, and in Your hand is power and might; and it lies in Your hand to make great and to strengthen everyone." Kingdom abundance isn't about having more but about trusting deeper. It's about knowing that God is both King and Provider and that His favor flows when His rule is recognized.

This is the goal of this session—to help you recognize His rule and reframe how you see your life, your provision, and your purpose. Because when you live as if God owns it all, you start to experience what it really means to live unleashed.

CONNECT | 10 MINUTES

Get this session started by choosing one or both of the following questions to discuss together as a group:

- What is something that spoke to you in last week's personal study that you would like to share with the group?

  — or —

- Think about a time when you were tempted to take control instead of trusting God as your provider. What did you learn through that experience about the difference between being a steward and acting like an owner?

WATCH | 25 MINUTES

Now watch the video for this session. Below is an outline of the key points covered during the teaching. Record any key concepts that stand out to you.

OUTLINE

I. God is the source—everything else is a resource.

   A. We often see ourselves as the owners when the truth is God alone owns it all.

   B. Psalm 24:1 and other Scriptures affirm God's full ownership of creation, wealth, and provision.

   C. Confusing resources with the Source disconnects us from kingdom living.

II. Kingdom stewardship requires the right perspective.

   A. We are house-sitters, not homeowners—entrusted with God's resources for His purpose.

   B. Ownership thinking leads to pride, entitlement, and misuse.

   C. True stewardship begins with humility and remembering who the King is.

III. Abundance flows through kingdom alignment.

   A. Living under God's rule releases provision, purpose, and peace.

   B. In Deuteronomy 8:11–14, Moses reminds the Israelites not to forget that God is the Source when the blessings come, because that is how the kingdom operates.

   C. Our attitude toward giving, receiving, and worship shifts when God is at the center.

IV. Kingdom blessings come with kingdom posture.

   A. Blessing is divine favor. It's where God gives us the opportunity to experience His goodness.

   B. In Matthew 5:3–11 (known as the Beatitudes) Jesus describes the kind of heart that God blesses.

     1. Humble, sorrowful (over falling short), and gentle (verses 3–5).

     2. Seeking (after righteousness), merciful, and pure (verses 6–8).

     3. Peacemaking and persecuted for the sake of righteousness (verses 9–11).

   C. Kingdom abundance includes comfort, inheritance, satisfaction, and reward.

V. Living in abundance means living under the King.

   A. Seeking the blessing without seeking the Blesser leads to emptiness.

   B. When you honor God as King, He releases His favor and fruit through your life.

   C. Kingdom abundance isn't about what you accumulate but about who you trust.

NOTES

DISCUSS | 35 MINUTES

Discuss what you just watched by answering the following questions.

1. Many of us think we are the conductors—that we are in charge of where we're going, how we're going to get there, and where we will end up. What is the danger with this kind of thinking? What is the reality of how much we are actually in charge over?

2. Read Psalm 50:10–11. What does the psalmist reveal about God's absolute authority over everything? How should this truth influence the way you hold your resources, manage your responsibilities, and pursue your goals?

3. God is the *source* and everything else is a *resource*. What are some resources in your life you've mistakenly treated as the source? How has that affected your trust in God?

4. Read Moses' words in Deuteronomy 8:16–18, which he spoke to the Israelites as they prepared to enter the promised land. What warnings and encouragements did he give to them? What were they to always remember about their time in the wilderness? How can remembering the true Source of your provision shape your attitude and decisions?

5. An important principle is that *kingdom blessing* flows from *kingdom posture*. Which of the Beatitudes from Matthew 5:3–11 speaks most to your current season—and why?

RESPOND | 10 MINUTES

When you recognize God is the source and everything else is just a resource, it changes how you live. Entitlement gives way to gratitude. Worry turns into worship. You stop clinging to what you've been given and start asking how God wants you to use it. Abundance doesn't begin with more stuff but with surrendered stewardship. When you align with God's kingdom, you open the door for His favor to flow through you. Reflect on these truths as you read the following passage and answer the questions that follow.

> "Bring the whole tithe into the storehouse, so that there may be food in My house, and put Me to the test now in this," says the LORD of armies, "if I do not open for you the windows of heaven and pour out for you a blessing until it overflows."
>
> **MALACHI 3:10**

Where in your life have you been tempted to rely on yourself rather than the Lord?

What would it look like this week to "bring the whole tithe into the storehouse"—to live as if everything you have belongs to the Lord and exists for His purposes?

PRAY | 10 MINUTES

As you close, thank God for all the ways He has provided for you. Ask the Holy Spirit to help you live with open hands and a kingdom mindset—to surrender your resources, your goals, and your influence to the One who gave them. Pray that you would remember the Source, rely on His provision, and reflect His generosity in the way you live, give, and lead. End by declaring your trust in God's rule and your desire to live as His steward, not your own master.

PERSONAL STUDY

In this week's group time, you discussed how abundance in God's kingdom isn't about *accumulation* but about *alignment*. When you stop living like the owner and start acting like a steward, you start to see that God is the Source and every-thing else is a resource. The readings in this personal study will challenge you to live like you actually believe that. You'll explore what the Bible says about God's ownership, your role as a steward, and how divine favor flows through a surren-dered life. You'll revisit David's prayer in 1 Chronicles 29:10–13 and see how Jesus reframed what it means to be blessed in the Sermon on the Mount.

Abundance isn't passive. It's a posture. It's choosing to depend on God when you want to depend on yourself. It's seeking to bless others when it would be easier to keep it all to yourself. It's choosing to trust the King, even when the resources in front of you seem small. As you engage in each of these personal studies, be sure to keep writing down your responses to the questions, as you will be given a few minutes to share your in-sights in the next session. If you are reading *Unleashed* along-side this study, first review chapters 7 and 9 of the book.

Study 1

ONLY STEWARDS

It's easy to forget whose name is on the title deed. We say things like "my money," "my house," and "my time." But in God's kingdom, those possessive pronouns don't hold up. This is because we don't *own* anything but *steward* everything.

David wrote, "The earth is the LORD's, and all it contains" (Psalm 24:1). That includes your paycheck, your breath, your calendar, and your creativity. It's all His. When you forget that, you slip into a dangerous mindset of entitlement—expecting blessings from God without recognizing His authority over them.

David understood this better than most. When preparing for the work of building the temple, he offered both leadership and wealth to the project, but his posture remained one of humility. In 1 Chronicles 29:14, he prayed, "But who am I and who are my people, that we should be able to offer as generously as this? For all things come from You, and from Your hand we have given to You."

That's not just a prayer of generosity. It's a declaration of theology. When you live like the owner, you feel the pressure to control, protect, and hoard. But when you live like a steward, you feel the freedom to trust, release, and obey. Ownership demands performance. Stewardship invites surrender.

This shift doesn't make you passive but purposeful. If God owns it all, then every dollar, hour, and talent you've been given carries kingdom potential. Your job is no longer just a job—it's a field God has placed under your care. Your home becomes a space for ministry. Your bank account becomes a tool for eternal impact. But this perspective requires a daily choice. The world will keep telling you to grab hold, take credit, and secure your own future. The kingdom tells you to hold loosely, give generously, and trust the King who never runs out of provision.

So today, take inventory . . . not of what you own but of what you've been entrusted with. Ask God to show you how to manage it with open hands and an aligned heart. You may be surprised at how much lighter life feels when you stop carrying what was never yours to own.

I. How tightly are you holding onto what God has asked you to steward? Consider your level of "tight-fistedness" in each of the areas of your life.

How firmly do you try to control your time?

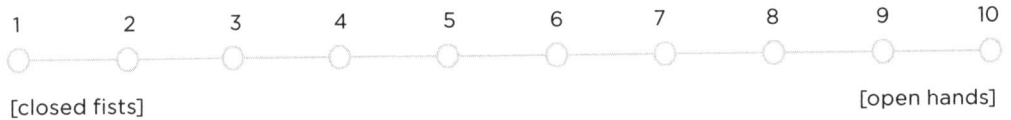

1	2	3	4	5	6	7	8	9	10
○	○	○	○	○	○	○	○	○	○

[closed fists]   [open hands]

How tightly do you try to grip onto money?

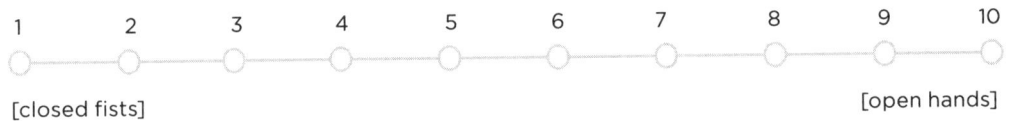

1	2	3	4	5	6	7	8	9	10
○	○	○	○	○	○	○	○	○	○

[closed fists]   [open hands]

How rigorously do you try to control your influence?

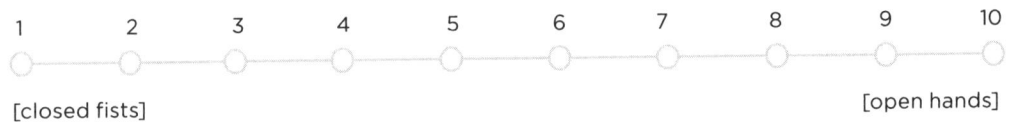

1	2	3	4	5	6	7	8	9	10
○	○	○	○	○	○	○	○	○	○

[closed fists]   [open hands]

2. Dwell on David's words in Psalm 24:1–2. If God owns *everything*, how should that shift the way you view your time, your finances, and your influence?

God wants us to get one thing straight: He made it all. He owns it all. As the owner, God does allow us to manage His resources. We call this *stewardship*. We are called and equipped to steward the time, talents, and treasures God places within our sphere of responsibility. What often happens, though, is that we confuse the resource with the Source. But the resources are merely the vehicles through which we receive what we need.[25]

3. Read Deuteronomy 10:14. Why is it so easy to forget that everything belongs to God—including your gifts, opportunities, and possessions? What's one area in your life where you might be acting more like the owner than the steward?

4. How do you define the difference between *owning* something and being *entrusted* with it? How should that shift your perspective on what you have? What would your life look like if you viewed your resources as part of God's kingdom instead of your personal kingdom?

David understood the gifts and offerings they gave to God came from God. In that sense, he was encouraging himself and the others to remain mindful of what they offered God. After all, if God was the supplier of their gifts to Him, what they gave Him should be something He wanted. As well, what they gave should come with a heart of gratitude for having been given the ability to give it at all. God is the owner of all we have. Even the tithe we give comes from Him. To give generously back to the One who has given to us evokes a heart of gratitude rather than a heart of pride or entitlement.[26]

5. Every gift you offer God came from Him. How should that influence the way you give? How should it impact the attitude you have when giving? What would it mean to give God something that He truly wants from you this week?

BLESSED TO BLESS

When God blesses you, He's not just trying to impress you but to work through you. Far too many Christians treat blessings like cul-de-sacs instead of conduits. They want God's goodness to stop with them rather than flow through them.

But in the kingdom, that's not how it works. When God called Abraham, He said, "I will make you into a great nation, and I will bless you, and make your name great; and you shall be a blessing" (Genesis 12:2). Did you catch that? "I will bless you . . . and you shall be a blessing." That's not two separate ideas. It's one statement with a divine purpose. God's blessings always come with an assignment. He doesn't hand out blessings for selfish consumption. He entrusts them for kingdom impact.

God may choose to bless you with money, time, wisdom, experience, or influence. But if that blessing stops with you, it will soon dry up. God never blesses for accumulation but for distribution. This is why Paul wrote to the believers in Corinth, "God is able to make all grace overflow to you, so that, always having all sufficiency in everything, you may have an abundance for every good deed" (2 Corinthians 9:8).

God pours in so you can pour out. Think of it like a water hose. A hose is only useful when it's connected to the source and open at the other end. As long as it stays aligned, the water flows. But the moment it is clamped shut, pressure builds and purpose is lost. In the same way, you can't clamp shut the blessings God intends you to use to reach someone else.

When you realize you're blessed to be a blessing, it transforms how you pray. You stop asking, "God, what can You give me?" and start asking, "God, what can You give through me?" You stop competing for provision and start cooperating in kingdom mission. That's the shift that unlocks abundance—not just in what you have but also in how you experience God's favor.

So if you're praying for blessing, get ready for assignment. If you're asking for overflow, prepare for God to show you who needs a drink. You are blessed to bless. That's how God gets the glory. And that's how you live unleashed.

1. Read Genesis 12:1–3. When you think about the blessings in your life—whether financial, relational, or spiritual—how have you used them to bless others? What might it look like to view your blessings as assignments?

2. Have you ever been tempted to treat God's blessings like a cul-de-sac—enjoying the gift without passing it on? What are some concerns (or even fears) you have when you consider opening the floodgates and seeking to bless others with what you have received?

To be blessed is to have all you need. It's a concept of divine favor where the provision of God flows both to you and through you with ease. To live the blessed life as a believer in Jesus Christ is to recognize Him as your Source and tap into His provision spiritually, emotionally, and physically. But many confuse the term *blessing* as being only about what they receive. They forget it has more to do with others than themselves. When God provides a blessing, He gives it so you can share it with others. If you use your blessings only for yourself, you are no longer living according to kingdom principles.[27]

3. Read 1 Timothy 6:17–19. Many of us think of *blessing* as being only about what we receive from God. But what does Paul say that those who are "rich in this present world" are to do with their resources?

The moment you become a cul-de-sac Christian rather than a conduit saint is the moment you start to self-limit your blessings. God is not going to continue to bless a self-centered saint. Knowing this, you can see how it would be wise to let God know how you plan to use the blessings He gives you in order to help others. When you go to God in prayer, asking for something from Him, be sure to let Him know how it will also benefit someone else. You are blessed to be a blessing.[28]

4. Read Acts 20:33–35. Paul spoke these words to the Ephesian elders as he was preparing to leave them and journey to Jerusalem. What does Paul say about his conduct? How might your prayers change this week if you asked God not just to bless you but to use you?

5. When you think about the blessings in your life, do you see them as rewards to enjoy or resources to steward? How would your daily choices shift if you truly believed that every blessing carries a kingdom purpose?

Study 3

BATTERIES INCLUDED

When you buy a new device, one of the first things you look for on the box is whether it says "batteries included." That tells you everything you need to know about its readiness—because a product without power is just a display. Sadly, far too many Christians are walking around like spiritual displays—shiny on the outside but powerless in the dark. They have the form of godliness but deny the power within (see 2 Timothy 3:5).

God did not send you into life empty. When He called you, He equipped you. When He saved you, He sealed you. When He filled you, He empowered you. If you belong to Christ, the Holy Spirit isn't optional equipment. You don't have to beg for Him. He came with the package! As Jesus said "You know Him because He remains with you and will be in you" (John 14:17).

That's "batteries included." But here's the catch: *Having* the Spirit and *walking* in the Spirit are two different things. The power has to be accessed. As Paul prayed, "[God] grant you, according to the riches of His glory, to be strengthened with power through His Spirit in the inner self" (Ephesians 3:16). Inner power produces outer stability. So, if you're not walking in the Spirit, don't be surprised if your life keeps stalling out.

When the great New York City blackout occurred back in 2003, only the buildings with internal generators stayed lit. The same goes for you. You don't need the world to keep your light on. You've got backup power. The kingdom of God is not sustained by external supply lines. It runs on the Spirit of the living God inside every believer.

The question isn't whether the power is there. The question is whether you're drawing from it. Have you flipped the switch of faith? Are you plugged into obedience? Is your prayer life functioning like a charger? Or have you been running on fumes?

You don't need a new source of strength. You need to use the one you've already been given. And once you do, it won't just sustain you—it will also empower you to bring light into the chaos around you. You were never meant to be a powerless believer. You were meant to brightly shine God's love with the batteries He's included.

1. Where do you feel like you're running low on spiritual power? What might be one way to reconnect with the strength God has already placed within you?

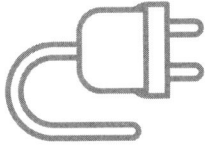

Running low in this area . . .   Could reconnect in this way . . .

2. Read Ephesians 3:14–19. What do you think Paul means when he says that you can be "strengthened with power through His Spirit in the inner self"?

Depending on God doesn't nullify your own gifts, abilities, and resources; it just shifts your focus from yourself to Him as your Source. When you recognize your insufficiency apart from Him, you receive the gift of the kingdom of heaven. That means God will give you the rule of the kingdom of heaven to operate in your life. Keep in mind, heaven's rule overrules whatever happens on earth. Thus, if you choose to be dependent upon earth for your needs, God will let you handle it on your own. But if you choose to be dependent upon God for your needs, He gives you the gift of heaven's rule on earth.[29]

3. It's easy to rely on your own talents, resources, or routines—especially if they have "worked" in the past. But spiritual authority doesn't come from self-sufficiency. Can you think of an area in your life where you've been trying to handle things on your own strength? What would it look like to intentionally shift that area back under God's rule and power?

When Jesus said, "Blessed are the poor in spirit, for theirs is the kingdom of heaven" (Matthew 5:3), He was describing those who recognize their own insufficiency. They recognize they don't have enough on their own. Those who are poor in spirit understand their own lack. They are self-aware concerning their need for God and His provision. Spiritual insufficiency means that if God doesn't do it, help you in it, provide for it—then you won't have enough to complete it on your own.[30]

4. Sometimes we want God's help without admitting how deeply we need it. But acknowledging our own lack is often the first step toward experiencing kingdom power. Where in your life have you been pretending to be "fine" while silently struggling? What would it look like to bring that place into the light and ask God to supply what you cannot?

5. Read Galatians 5:25–26. You already have access to the Spirit's power. The question is whether you are actively walking in it. In what ways might you be running on "spiritual autopilot" instead of staying plugged into God's presence? What would change this week if you flipped the switch of faith and fully relied on His power within you?

CATCH UP AND READ AHEAD

Connect with a fellow group member this week and discuss some of the key insights from this session. Use any of the following prompts to guide your discussion.

- What shifted your perspective most in this session—whether that was about ownership, stewardship, or what it means to truly live in abundance? How has that impacted your view of God's role in your daily decisions?
- Where in your life have you confused a resource for the Source? How has that shaped the way you handle success, struggle, or provision?
- One theme from this session was living with "batteries included"—drawing from the Holy Spirit's power that is already present within you. What helps you stay connected to that power? What tends to drain it?
- God blesses us not just to enjoy abundance but to share it. How does seeing yourself as a conduit rather than a container challenge you?
- Looking ahead, in what area of your life do you want to grow in kingdom alignment—your time, your influence, your finances, or something else? What's one step you can take this week to move in that direction?

Take a moment to revisit any study or reflection questions from earlier sessions that you haven't yet finished. As you do, jot down any fresh insights, moments of clarity, or ways you've seen growth in your thinking, habits, or spiritual posture.

Read chapter 10 in *Unleashed* before the next group gathering. Make a note of anything in those chapters that stands out to you or encourages you.

BEFORE GROUP MEETING	Read chapter 10 in *Unleashed* Read the Welcome section (page 102)
GROUP MEETING	Discuss the Connect questions Watch the video teaching for session 6 Discuss the questions that follow as a group Do the closing exercise and pray (pages 102–106)
STUDY 1	Complete the personal study (pages 109–112)
STUDY 2	Complete the personal study (pages 113–116)
STUDY 3	Complete the personal study (pages 117–120)
WRAP IT UP	Connect with someone in your group Complete any unfinished personal studies (page 121) Connect with your group about the next study you want to go through together

LEAVING A MARK

[Impact]

"Your light must shine before people in such a way that they may see your good works, and glorify your Father who is in heaven."

MATTHEW 5:16

WELCOME | READ ON YOUR OWN

You weren't put on this planet to take up space. You were placed here to make a statement. In this final session, we're talking about what it means to leave a kingdom mark. Not just a memory, or a moment, but a visible, verbal, Spirit-filled impact that makes heaven known on earth. You weren't saved to sit. You were saved to shine.

Remember the term "kingdom agenda" is defined as the visible manifestation of the comprehensive rule of God over every area of life. The kingdom agenda involves God's will revealed in real-time situations. Advancing His kingdom agenda means committing your time, talents, and treasures to the revelation of His will on earth. When you do this, you make a Spirit-filled impact and leave a kingdom mark.

Peter writes, "You are a chosen people, a royal priesthood, a holy nation, a people for God's own possession" (1 Peter 2:9). That's not just a title; it's a calling. The purpose? "So that you may proclaim the excellencies of Him who called you out of darkness into His marvelous light." If God pulled you out, He expects you to speak up.

We're living in a day of silent saints—Christians who are hiding their light while the world turns up the volume. God is not looking for undercover believers. He's looking for visible representatives. People who reflect their true citizenship not in whispers but with bold, loving, unmistakable clarity. Heaven is counting on you to show up. You've been called to the field. So lace up. Speak out. It's time to leave a mark.

CONNECT | 10 MINUTES

Get this session started by choosing one or both of the following questions to discuss together as a group:

- What is something that spoke to you in last week's personal study that you would like to share with the group?

— or —

- Think of a time you had an opportunity to speak up or live out your faith. Did you step into it or hold back? What influenced your response?

WATCH | 25 MINUTES

Now watch the video for this session. Below is an outline of the key points covered during the teaching. Record any key concepts that stand out to you.

OUTLINE

I. Your identity shapes your impact.
   A. Peter reminds believers they are a chosen people, royal priests, and holy representatives of God's kingdom (1 Peter 2:9).
   B. Knowing who you are in Christ should change how you live and what you declare.
   C. Kingdom living requires your posture to match your position.

II. You've been called to proclaim.
   A. You are to proclaim the excellencies of the One who has called you out of darkness into light.
   B. Silent Christianity contradicts visible faith. Believers in Christ must speak truth in love, clearly and unapologetically.
   C. Your witness is both verbal and visible, pointing others to God's glory.

III. Your life is your platform.
   A. Good deeds are not just good things—they're God-things that reflect your faith.
   B. A good work is an action that benefits others and connects to your belief.
   C. Faith and works must be fully integrated to make a kingdom impact.

IV. You are a citizen of another realm.
   A. Your primary identity is tied to heaven, not earth.
   B. Just as Roman colonies lived under Rome's rule, you live under heaven's authority on earth.
   C. Don't lose your kingdom identity trying to blend into the culture around you.

V. God expects you to leave a mark.
   A. Kingdom representation isn't optional—it's your calling.
   B. If you were accused of being a full-time representative of Jesus, the evidence should be overwhelming.
   C. It's time to live like you've been sent—to make heaven known through your words and works.

NOTES

DISCUSS | 35 MINUTES

Discuss what you just watched by answering the following questions.

1. Your identity in Christ includes being chosen, royal, and holy. How should embracing that identity shape the way you approach your daily decisions and relationships?

2. Read Philippians 3:18–21. How does Paul describe those who have their minds set on "earthly things"? Where does he say your true citizenship should lie— and what challenges do you face when trying to live according to those standards in an earthly culture?

3. "Good works" can be defined as actions that benefit others and bring glory to God. How do you personally distinguish between "good things" and "good works" in your life?

4. Read Jesus' words in Matthew 5:13–16. What does He say is the role of salt and light in the world? How can you live more boldly and visibly as a kingdom representative in your current setting?

5. Think of a specific area in your life where you've stayed silent about your faith— maybe out of fear, discomfort, or doubt. What would it look like to speak up, act boldly, or "leave a mark" in that space this week? What initial step could you take to do this?

RESPOND | 10 MINUTES

You weren't just saved to go to heaven. You were saved to represent heaven on earth. While God isn't looking for perfect people to fulfill this mission, He is looking for faithful ones who will speak up when it's easier to stay quiet and live with integrity when no one is watching. When your life reflects Christ in both word and actions, people won't just notice you but be pointed to Jesus. Reflect on this as you read the following passage and answer the questions that follow:

> Beloved, I urge you as foreigners and strangers to abstain from fleshly lusts, which wage war against the soul. Keep your behavior excellent among the Gentiles, so that in the thing in which they slander you as evildoers, they may because of your good deeds, as they observe them, glorify God on the day of visitation.
>
> **1 PETER 2:11–12**

Why does Peter instruct followers of Jesus to "abstain from fleshly lusts" and "keep your behavior excellent"?

When people see your life—your words, work, and witness—what do they see? How can you more intentionally align your public presence with your kingdom identity?

PRAY | 10 MINUTES

Close out this Bible study by thanking God for calling you out of darkness and into His light. Pray for courage to live with conviction, humility to walk in obedience, and strength to speak the name of Jesus with love and confidence wherever He leads. Ask God to make your life a living testimony so your words and actions point people to the One who saved you.

PERSONAL STUDY

You weren't just saved to sit. You were saved to *serve*. God didn't pull you out of darkness just to make you comfortable in the light. He called you, chose you, and placed you where you are to represent Him and to leave a mark that lasts. The goal is not just about being "a good person" but living like a kingdom ambassador—a visible representative of heaven here on earth. You've been placed in a dark world to shine. You've been called out so you can speak up. You're not here to blend in with the crowd. You're here to bring clarity to the chaos.

As you conclude this study, you'll explore what it means to be a kingdom influencer—a cultural "fifth columnist" who lives in this world but is loyal to another realm. You'll be challenged to live out your citizenship from above while walking boldly here. And you'll discover that real impact doesn't come from having a title but from living out your kingdom calling. So let's go deep. Let's get clear. And let's live unleashed. Remember to continue recording your responses, insights, and key takeaways as you work through these exercises. If you are reading *Unleashed* alongside this study, first review chapter 10 of the book.

MARKED FOR MORE

You're not ordinary. You're not random. And you're definitely not forgotten. If you've placed your faith in Jesus Christ, you've been marked—set apart—for something far greater than survival. You've been marked for *impact*.

In 1 Peter 2:9–10, God makes it clear who you are: "You are a chosen people, a royal priesthood, a holy nation . . . you once were not a people, but now you are the people of God; you had not received mercy, but now you have received mercy."

That's not just spiritual niceties. That's kingdom identity. And it comes with kingdom responsibility. You weren't saved just to get into heaven. You were saved to bring heaven's influence down to earth. You're royalty. You're priestly. You're part of the people of God. You've been handpicked by Him to proclaim His goodness, display His glory, and live out His values in a world that's lost its way. Your life isn't random. It's a kingdom calling in motion.

Many Christians, unfortunately, forget who they are. They walk around slouching in their identity, quiet in their faith, and passive in their mission. But when you understand that you're *chosen*, it straightens your back and lifts up your chin. It reminds you that your identity was assigned by heaven and not by the culture, not by your past, and definitely not by your performance. After all, God didn't just save you from something. He saved you *for* something. As Paul says, "We are His workmanship, created in Christ Jesus for good works, which God prepared beforehand so that we would walk in them" (Ephesians 2:10).

You were handcrafted for kingdom assignments. You were designed to do more than just breathe air and make it to the weekend. You were made to proclaim Christ with clarity and serve His purpose with joy. That means you can't hide in the shadows. You weren't meant to be a secret-agent Christian. You were called to go public, not only with your words but also with your witness and your works.

Don't live beneath your identity. You're not who the world says you are or who your past says you are. You are who God says you are. And He says you are chosen.

I. Read Jeremiah 1:5 and Psalm 139:13–14. If God knew you and set you apart before you were even born, how should that reshape your view of what today holds? Where might you be living like you're random or invisible instead of chosen and commissioned?

2. Read Luke 8:16–17. If your life was the only glimpse of Jesus someone saw today, what kind of picture would that person walk away with? How can you put the light of God "on a lampstand" and reflect it more boldly in the places you've been tempted to dim it down?

Peter addressed his readers as a "chosen people" and a "royal priesthood" (1 Peter 2:9). In using two descriptive terms in "royal priesthood," Peter married two concepts. Royalty has to do with kingship. Priesthood has to do with duty to God. A priest serves as an intermediary between God and man. Peter followed up these descriptions by reminding us that we are "a people for God's own possession." We have been chosen to reflect and represent God's kingdom on earth under His rule. When we do that, we unleash all He has in store to support the advancement of His kingdom. This reality ought to change how we show up in life. Far too many believers live an "under the circumstances" sort of existence. But when you realize you are chosen, appointed, and supplied with all you need to carry out God's kingdom authority on earth, it ought to change your perspective not only toward yourself but also toward your circumstances.[31]

3. Think about these concepts that Peter presents of believers in Christ being both *royalty* and members of the *priesthood.*

What would change in your day-to-day attitude if you truly believed you were a "priest"—an intermediary between God and people?

What would change if you truly believed that you were "royalty"—a member of God's own family with full access to the King?

In what areas have you been living "under the circumstances" instead of walking in your kingdom identity?

4. You've been both "chosen" (1 Peter 2:9) and "created in Christ" (Ephesians 2:10)—set apart for God's purpose and prepared for His assignments. How does holding these two truths together reshape your sense of identity and mission? What good works might be waiting for you to step forward in faith and carry them out?

You are a kingdom disciple living as a kingdom servant while making a kingdom impact that will resonate throughout all time. And you do this through proclaiming "the excellencies of Him who has called you out of darkness into His marvelous light" (1 Peter 2:9). You are to be a proclaimer of Christ. A more contemporary term would be *kingdom influencer.* You are to use your status, time, talent, and treasures to influence others for God's glory and the greater good of all. You are to serve notice on the culture that Jesus is here and His kingdom is alive and well. As a kingdom influencer, your intention should be that of proclaiming the gospel to a lost world and bringing glory to God.[32]

5. Read 2 Corinthians 5:20-21. If you are God's ambassador—His official representative on earth—how are you reflecting His message in your conversations, habits, and relationships? How could you more intentionally align with your role as a kingdom influencer?

Study 2

FAITH THAT SHOWS

Faith is more than a belief in your head. It's a conviction in your heart that shows up in your hands and feet. James said, "Prove yourselves doers of the word, and not just hearers who deceive themselves" (1:22). If you say you believe it, then live like it.

Kingdom faith was never meant to be hidden. It was meant to be on full display. Too many believers today are walking around with silent faith. Jesus didn't call us out of darkness so we would hide in the shadows. He called us into the light so we could shed light to a world in darkness. As He said, "Your light must shine before people in such a way that they may see your good works, and glorify your Father who is in heaven" (Matthew 5:16).

That's the point. Your good works are not about applause. They are about reflection. They reflect the heart of the Father to a world that desperately needs to see Him.

But keep in mind, you shouldn't confuse good *works* with good *things*. Anybody can do good things. The world is full of philanthropists and humanitarians who do good stuff all the time. But good works are different. Good works are biblically driven, God-centered acts of service that flow from your relationship with Christ. They're good because they are rooted in truth and powered by the Spirit. What's more, they always point back to God for the glory.

When you serve someone, love someone, forgive someone, speak truth, or meet a need in Jesus' name, that's a good work. When people see your actions and give glory to God instead of giving credit to you, that's a good work. If your faith hasn't made it yet to your feet, your schedule, your wallet, or your relationships, it's time to bring it out into the open. Because faith that stays private never reaches its full potential. You've got to move it from belief to behavior. From theory to testimony. From invisible to impactful.

So let the people around you see what you believe. Let your light shine boldly. Let your faith walk say something much louder than your faith talk. Because if you're truly connected to Christ, it really ought to show up and show out for Jesus.

113

I. Read James 2:14–17. What connection does James make between *faith* and *good works*? Where in your life is your faith most visible—and where is it hiding in the shadows?

2. It's easy to confuse good *things* with good *works*. The difference is in who gets the glory. Think back on something kind or sacrificial you've done recently. Did that act point people to *Jesus* or just reflect well on *you*? If it's the latter, what would it look like for you to make your faith more God-centered and less self-impressive?

The term *fifth column* refers to individuals in a foreign situation who act on behalf of their own loyalties. They operate on behalf of a country other than the one they are currently in. God also has an embedded group of "fifth columnists"—His kingdom representatives who have been saved not only for the purpose of going to heaven when they die but also for representing and advancing His kingdom agenda on earth. As a reminder, the "kingdom agenda" can be defined as the visible manifestation of the comprehensive rule of God over every area of life. The kingdom agenda involves God's will revealed in real-time situations. Advancing His kingdom agenda means intentionally committing your time, talents, and treasures to the revelation of His will on earth.[33]

3. Your faith wasn't meant to be tucked away for heaven—it was designed to bring God's rule to earth right now. What are some of the talents you could use to intentionally show God's will in action this week? What about your time, your talents, or your resources?

You must live as a visible, verbal follower of Jesus Christ, not as a secret-agent Christian. Now, you are to do this lovingly and with compassion and sensitivity, but you are to stand for what you know to be true. You are not to be ashamed of the gospel. You are not to be ashamed of God taking you out of darkness and placing you in the light. People should see your good works and hear your good words.[34]

4. What does it mean to live as a "visible" and "verbal" follower of Jesus? What does it look like for your faith to be both bold *and* loving in your everyday conversations and choices?

5. Read Colossians 3:17. Visible faith isn't about performance but about purpose. Your actions are meant to reflect Jesus, not represent you. So take inventory. If someone watched your *schedule*, your *speech*, your *spending*, and your *service*, what would they conclude about your faith? Would they see a clear

connection between what you believe and how you behave? Take a moment to assess each of these areas of your life.

My schedule . . .

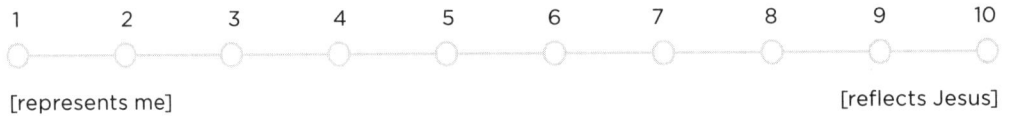

[represents me]   [reflects Jesus]

My speech . . .

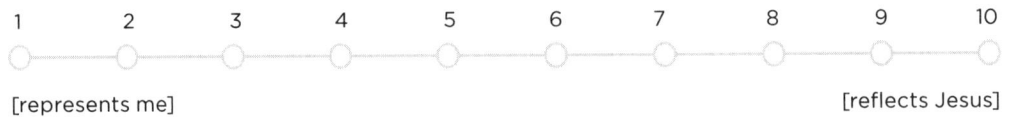

[represents me]   [reflects Jesus]

My spending . . .

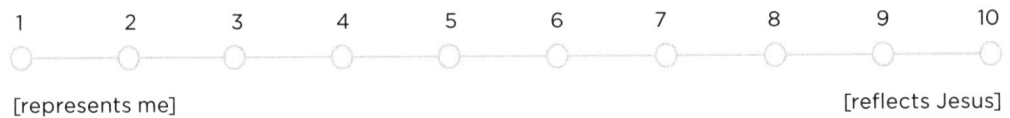

[represents me]   [reflects Jesus]

My service . . .

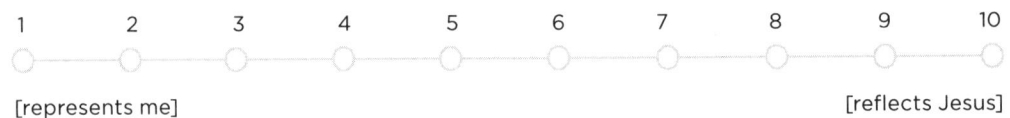

[represents me]   [reflects Jesus]

In which specific area could your light shine more intentionally for God's glory?

Study 3

KINGDOM OVER CULTURE

You can't represent two kingdoms at the same time. Eventually, one will have your loyalty. As Jesus said, "No one can serve two masters; for either he will hate the one and love the other, or he will be devoted to one and despise the other" (Matthew 6:24).

Jesus was speaking in this verse about wealth—about serving God or money. But the truth applies to every area of life. We live in a time when culture is loud and truth is optional. But the kingdom of God is not a cultural suggestion. It is a divine rule. And those who belong to it are called to live under its authority.

Your ultimate allegiance is not to a flag, a party, a background, or a trend. Your allegiance is to the throne of God. And His rule must override every other voice. Culture changes with the wind, but God's kingdom never moves. When the world shifts, the Word stands. When society redefines truth, the kingdom reasserts it.

Believers in Christ are called to live differently: "Do not be conformed to this world, but be transformed by the renewing of your mind" (Romans 12:2). That means you don't just resist the culture; rather, you renew your thinking to reflect the rule of Christ. To live kingdom over culture is to let heaven's values shape how you think, how you spend, how you speak, how you forgive, how you lead, and how you love. It's not just about morality. It's about allegiance. It's about refusing to be discipled by the world and choosing instead to be shaped by the King.

You've been called to be more than a cultural observer. You're a kingdom ambassador—a living representative of heaven in a divided world. You weren't saved to survive but to serve here by shining and reflecting the light of God. So let the world see where you stand. Let your values run deeper than current social media posts and trending topics. Let your life speak louder than the noise.

Let your works glorify God. The kingdom is here. It's in you. The King is calling. The culture is watching. So live fully alive and fully unleashed.

1. Read Hebrews 11:8–10. How is Abraham described in this passage? Where in your life are you most tempted to blend in with the world instead of living as a bold citizen of heaven?

2. Read Ephesians 4:20–24. What does Paul say in this passage about the importance of having your mind shaped by God's kingdom truth rather than cultural trends? What step could you take this week to renew your mind and live in a way that reflects the true rule of Christ?

Jesus isn't handing out dual-citizenship opportunities. He wants you to know you are a citizen of heaven on a visa to earth. You are simply passing through this land, because your homeland is above. If you forget this, you will become too attached to earth, even to the point that the world's wisdom and values will influence your decisions. In short, the world will own you, not God. As a citizen of heaven, your allegiance is to God.[35]

3. How does this idea that you are on a "visa" to earth help you understand your purpose here? What does it mean for you to be an *ambassador* for Christ?

Whatever gets in the way of your honoring Christ and His kingdom principles becomes an impediment to unleashing His presence in your life. You are to live as a *Christian* first, not as a citizen of your nation, or as your racial identity, or your political affiliation first. Far too many believers live powerless Christian lives because they fail to understand this basic foundational life principle. If and when you do not know who you are and whose you are, the enemy will seek to redefine you according to his goals, strategies, and values. As a result, you will live a double-minded and confused existence, accomplishing little for yourself, God's kingdom, and the greater good of all.[36]

4. Where have cultural labels or political identities competed with your identity in Christ? What truth do you need to reclaim to live with undivided allegiance to God's kingdom?

5. Read Matthew 6:33 and Galatians 2:20. You've spent six weeks learning what it means to live under God's rule, aligned with His Spirit, empowered by His authority, and defined by His truth. Now that you've seen what kingdom living looks like, how will you respond? What specific shift—whether in priority, perspective, or practice—do you sense God calling you to make so that His kingdom comes more fully in and through you?

Serving God means staying in close contact with Him so you can hear Him and know what to do and say every moment. It means drawing near to Him in order to tap into His grace, majesty, and power. Living as a kingdom influencer requires you to wear His brand and reflect His image to others. When you do that, He will empower you to be seen and recognized by others as His follower. His kingdom power is closer to you than you may think. What's more, He's given you the insight into what it takes to access it. Doing so is up to you. God has made His kingdom blessings, grace, and might available to you. In fact, the kingdom of God is at hand. Or, rather, the kingdom of God is in your hands. It's up to you to unleash it.[37]

WRAP IT UP

Connect with a fellow group member this week and discuss some of the key insights from this session. Use any of the following prompts to guide your discussion.

- What from this final session challenged or inspired you the most—whether in the teaching, the Scriptures, or the devotional reflections? How does it connect with what God has been stirring in you throughout the study?
- An emphasis in this session was living out your kingdom identity boldly. What is one area where you've been silent or hesitant to represent Christ? What would it look like to step forward in faith now?
- Over the past six weeks, you've look at themes including power, authority, alignment, stewardship, blessing, and boldness. Which of these themes has been the most personally transformative for you? Why?
- The kingdom of God isn't just something you're waiting for but is something you live out right now. How can your words, habits, or relationships more clearly reflect your heavenly citizenship moving forward?
- Thinking back through all six sessions, where have you seen the greatest shift in your mindset or your mission? How do you want to keep growing as a kingdom influencer in the days ahead?

Use this time to go back and complete any of the study and reflection questions from previous days that you weren't able to finish. Make a note of any revelations you've had and reflect on any growth or personal insights you've gained.

Finally, discuss with your group what studies you might want to go through next and when you will plan on meeting together again to study God's Word.

LEADER'S GUIDE

Thank you for your willingness to lead your group through this study! What you have chosen to do is valuable and will make a difference in the lives of others. *Unleashed* is a six-session Bible study built around video content and small-group interaction. As the group leader, imagine yourself as the host of a party. Your job is to take care of your guests by managing the details so that when your guests arrive, they can focus on one another and on the interaction around the topic for that session.

Your role as the group leader is not to answer all the questions or reteach the content—the video, book, and study guide will do most of that work. Your job is to guide the experience and cultivate your small group into a connected and engaged community. This will make it a place for members to process, question, and reflect—not necessarily to receive more instruction. There are several elements in this leader's guide that will help you as you structure your study and reflection time, so be sure to follow along and take advantage of each one.

BEFORE YOU BEGIN

Before your first meeting, make sure the group members have a copy of this study guide. Alternately, you can hand out the study guides at your first meeting and give the members some time to look over the material and ask any preliminary questions. Also, make sure that the group members are aware they have access to the streaming videos at any time by following the instructions provided with this guide. During your first meeting, ask the members to provide their names, phone numbers, and email addresses so that you can keep in touch.

Generally, the ideal size for a group is eight to ten people, which will ensure that everyone has enough time to participate in discussions. If you have more people, break up the main group into smaller subgroups. Encourage those who show up at the first meeting to commit to attending the duration of the study, as this will help the group members get to know one another, create stability for the group, and help you know how best to prepare to lead the participants through the material.

Each session begins with an opening reflection in the Welcome section. The questions that follow in the Connect section serve as icebreakers to get the group members thinking about the topic. In the rest of the study, it's generally not a good idea to have everyone answer every question—a free-flowing discussion is more desirable. But with the icebreaker question, you can go around the circle and ask each person to respond. Encourage shy people to share, but don't force them.

At your first meeting, let the group members know each session also contains a personal study section they can use to continue to engage with the content until the next meeting. While doing this section is optional, it will help cement the concepts presented during the group study time so they can better understand what it means to be *unleashed* in God's kingdom.

Let them know that if they choose to do so, they can watch the video for the next session by accessing the streaming code provided with this study guide. Invite them to bring any questions and insights to your next meeting, especially if they had a breakthrough moment or didn't understand something.

PREPARATION FOR EACH SESSION

As the leader, there are a few things you should do to best prepare for each meeting:

- **Read through the session.** This will help you become more familiar with the content and know how to structure the discussion times.
- **Decide how the videos will be used.** Determine whether you want the members to watch the videos ahead of time (again, via the streaming access code provided with this study guide) or together as a group.
- **Decide which questions you want to discuss.** Based on the length of your group discussions, you may not be able to get through all the questions. So look over the discussion questions provided in each session and mark which ones you definitely want to cover.
- **Be familiar with the questions you want to discuss.** When the group meets, you'll be watching the clock, so make sure you are familiar with the questions you have selected.
- **Pray for your group.** Pray for your group members and ask God to lead them as they study His Word and listen to His Spirit.

In many cases, there will be no one "right" answer to the questions. Answers will vary, especially when the group members are sharing their personal experiences.

STRUCTURING THE DISCUSSION TIME

You will need to determine with your group how long you want your meetings to last so that you can plan your time accordingly. Suggested times for each section have been provided in this study guide, and if you adhere to these times, your group will meet for ninety minutes. However, many groups like to meet for two hours. If this describes your particular group, follow the times listed in the right-hand column of the chart given below.

Section	90 Minutes	120 Minutes
CONNECT (discuss one or more of the opening questions for the session)	15 minutes	20 minutes
WATCH (watch the teaching material together and take notes)	20 minutes	20 minutes
DISCUSS (discuss the study questions you selected ahead of time)	35 minutes	50 minutes
RESPOND (write down key takeaways)	10 minutes	15 minutes
PRAY (pray together and dismiss)	10 minutes	15 minutes

As the group leader, it is up to you to keep track of the time and to keep things on schedule. You might want to set a timer for each segment so that both you and the group members know when the time is up. (There are some good phone apps for timers that play a gentle chime or other pleasant sound instead of a disruptive noise.)

Don't be concerned if group members are quiet or slow to share. People are often quiet when they are pulling together their ideas, and this might be a new experience for some of them. Just ask a question and let it hang in the air until someone shares. You can then say, "Thank you. What about others? What came to you when you watched that portion of the teaching?"

GROUP DYNAMICS

Leading a group through *Unleashed* will be highly rewarding both to you and your group members. But you still may encounter challenges along the way! Discussions can get off track. Group members may not be sensitive to the needs and ideas of others. Some might worry that they will be expected to talk about matters that make them feel awkward. Others may express comments that result in disagreements.

To help ease this strain on you and the group, consider the following ground rules:

- When someone raises a question or comment that is off the main topic, suggest you deal with it another time, or, if you feel led to go in that direction, let the group know that you will be spending some time discussing it.
- If someone asks a question that you don't know how to answer, admit it and move on. At your discretion, feel free to invite group members to comment on questions that call for personal experience.
- If you find that one or two people are dominating the discussion time, direct a few questions to others in the group. Outside the main group time, ask the more dominating members to help you draw out the quieter ones. Work to make them part of the solution instead of part of the problem.
- When a disagreement occurs, encourage the group members to process the matter in love. Encourage those on opposite sides to restate what they heard the other side say about the matter, and then invite each side to evaluate if that perception is accurate. Lead the group in examining other passages related to the topic and look for common ground.

When any of these issues arise, encourage your group members to follow these words from Scripture: "Love one another" (John 13:34); "If possible, so far as it depends on you, be at peace with all people" (Romans 12:18); "Whatever is true . . . honorable . . . right . . . pure . . . lovely . . . commendable . . . if there is any excellence and if anything worthy of praise, think about these things" (Philippians 4:8); and, "Everyone must be quick to hear, slow to speak, and slow to anger" (James 1:19). This will make your group time more rewarding and beneficial for everyone who attends.

Thank you for taking the time to lead your group. You are making a difference in your members' lives and having an impact on their journey toward a better understanding of how to unleash the kingdom of God in the world around them.

NOTES

1. Tony Evans, *Unleashed: Releasing God's Glorious Kingdom in and Through You* (W Publishing, 2025), 2-3.
2. Evans, *Unleashed*, 22.
3. Evans, *Unleashed*, 34.
4. Evans, *Unleashed*, 30.
5. Evans, *Unleashed*, 41.
6. Evans, *Unleashed*, 172-173.
7. Evans, *Unleashed*, 48.
8. Evans, *Unleashed*, 50-51.
9. Evans, *Unleashed*, 47-48.
10. Evans, *Unleashed*, 48.
11. Evans, *Unleashed*, 55.
12. Evans, *Unleashed*, 55-56.
13. Evans, *Unleashed*, 64, 66.
14. Evans, *Unleashed*, 73.
15. Evans, *Unleashed*, 68.
16. Evans, *Unleashed*, 71.
17. Evans, *Unleashed*, 90.
18. Evans, *Unleashed*, 91, 93.
19. Evans, *Unleashed*, 104-105.
20. Evans, *Unleashed*, 145, 147.
21. Evans, *Unleashed*, 106-107.
22. Evans, *Unleashed*, 149.
23. Evans, *Unleashed*, 115.
24. Evans, *Unleashed*, 153-154.
25. Evans, *Unleashed*, 122-123.
26. Evans, *Unleashed*, 126.
27. Evans, *Unleashed*, 163-164.
28. Evans, *Unleashed*, 164.
29. Evans, *Unleashed*, 166.
30. Evans, *Unleashed*, 166.
31. Evans, *Unleashed*, 181-182.
32. Evans, *Unleashed*, 185.
33. Evans, *Unleashed*, 178-179.
34. Evans, *Unleashed*, 189.
35. Evans, *Unleashed*, 183-184.
36. Evans, *Unleashed*, 183.
37. Evans, *Unleashed*, 191-192.

ABOUT DR. TONY EVANS

Dr. Tony Evans is the founding pastor of Oak Cliff Bible Fellowship in Dallas, founder and president of The Urban Alternative, former chaplain of the NBA Dallas Mavericks and the NFL Dallas Cowboys, and author of more than 150 books, booklets, and Bible studies. The first African American to earn a doctorate of theology at Dallas Theological Seminary, he has been named one of the twelve most effective preachers in the English-speaking world by Baylor University.

Dr. Evans holds the honor of writing and publishing the first full-Bible commentary and study Bible by an African American. His radio broadcast, *The Alternative with Dr. Tony Evans*, can be heard on more than 1,200 radio outlets. He launched the Tony Evans Training Center (TETC) in 2017, an online learning platform providing quality, seminary-style courses for a fraction of the cost to any person in any place. The TETC currently has over fifty courses to choose from and has a student population of more than 2,000.

Dr. Evans was married to Lois, his wife and ministry partner of more than fifty years, until Lois transitioned to glory in late 2019. They are the proud parents of four, grandparents of thirteen, and great-grandparents of four. In November 2023, Dr. Evans married Carla Evans. For more information, visit **tonyevans.org**.